2022 ROMAN REPLIES & CLSA ADVISORY OPINIONS

DONNA MILLER, JD, JCL
EDITOR, ROMAN REPLIES

VERY REV. PATRICK COONEY, OSB, JCL
REV. MSGR. MICHAEL A. SOUCKAR, JCD
EDITORS, ADVISORY OPINIONS

Canon Law Society of America

ISBN 978-1-932208-64-1
ISSN 1543-4230
SAN 237-6296

Unless otherwise noted, all canons quoted are from the *Code of Canon Law, Latin-English Edition* (Washington, DC: Canon Law Society of America, 2020) and the *Code of Canons of the Eastern Churches, Latin-English Edition* (Washington, DC: Canon Law Society of America, 2001).

Printed in the United States of America.

Canon Law Society of America
415 Michigan Avenue NE, Suite 101
Washington, DC 20017-4502
admin@clsa.org

TABLE OF CONTENTS

Foreword....5

ROMAN REPLIES 2022

Introductory Note....9

CANONS 220, 1077, 1099, 1457; AND *DIGNITAS CONNUBII* ART. 251: Regarding the Application of Article 251 of *Dignitas connubii* on the Imposition of a *Vetitum*....11

CANONS 587 §2; 624 §1; AND 627 §1: Regarding Changes in the Constitution of a Religious Institute and Request for Immediate Implementation....14

CANON 587: Regarding Extension of Term of Office for Interim Superior General Following Death of Superior General....19

CANON 1295: Regarding a Bishop's Request that Parishes Share in Funding the Monetary Obligation Arising from the Settlement of Sexual Abuse Cases....20

TRADITIONIS CUSTODES ART. 3 §2: Regarding a Request for Dispensation....29

CCEO CANON 916 §5; *DIGNITAS CONNUBII* ART. 16, §1: Competency of Latin Tribunals Extended to Eritrean Church in Canada....32

OTHER VATICAN DOCUMENTS

Rescriptum ex Audientia Ss.Mi, October 11, 2021: Norms Regarding Delicts Reserved to the Congregation for the Doctrine of the Faith....36

Address of His Holiness Pope Francis to the Officials of the Tribunal of the Roman Rota for the Inauguration of the Judicial Year....45

Apostolic Letter Issued *Motu Proprio* of the Supreme Pontiff Francis *Competentias Quasdam Decernere* Introducing Changes to Some Norms of the Code of Canon Law and the Code of Canons of the Eastern Churches....50

Apostolic Letter Issued *Motu Proprio:* The Supreme Pontiff Francis Revised Book VI by Wwhich Can. 695 §1 of the Code of Canon Law Is Modified 56

Rescriptum Ex Audientia Ss.Mi: Rescript of the Holy Father Francis Regarding the Derogation from Can. 588 §2 *CIC* 57

Rescriptum Ex Audientia Ss.Mi: Rescritto Del Santo Padre Francesco Circa Le Associazioni Pubbliche Di Fedeli In Itinere 58

ADVISORY OPINIONS 2022

Introductory Note 61

CANON 128: Responsibility and Liability for Repair of Harm to Abuse Victims (Daly) 63

CANON 694: *Ipso Facto* Dismissal For Illegitimate Absence (D. Miller) 71

CANONS 764 (CIC/17) AND 872, 873 (CIC/83): Regarding the Recording of Baptismal Sponsors (Mangan) 79

CANONS 843 §1 AND 915: Regarding Reception of Holy Communion by Individuals in a Same-Sex Civil Marriage (Quinan) 81

CANONS 843 §1 AND 915: Regarding Reception of Holy Communion by Transgender and Non-Binary Individuals (Quinan) 88

CANONS 1101 §1; 1127 §3; 1156-1160: Can Couples Renew Their Wedding "Vows?" (B. Miller) 101

CANON 1262: Restrictions on Fundraising Imposed by an Episcopal Vicar on the Fundraising Ability of a Religious Institute (Pietrzyk) 105

CANONS 1277 AND 1295: Acts of Extraordinary Administration by Diocesan Bishop and Transactions through which the Patrimonial Condition of a Juridic Person Can Be Worsened (Paprocki) 110

TRADITIONIS CUSTODES: Concerning the Sacramental Validity of the 1962 Liturgical Texts (Marcello) 113

Contributors 117

Foreword

The Canon Law Society of America (CLSA) publishes annually *Roman Replies and CLSA Advisory Opinions* for canonists and those seeking a clearer understanding of the *praxis legis* of the Catholic Church. The combination of these two services, begun in 1984, continues to serve as useful resources for those involved in the application of canonical discipline.

The compilation of materials for *Roman Replies 2022* was guided by Donna Miller, Executive Coordinator of the CLSA and an *ex officio* member of the CLSA Publications Advisory Board. The collection of entries in this issue, when viewed in conjunction with previous volumes, assists the reader both in understanding recent developments in the law and in identifying current trends in the praxis of the Roman Curia.

The selection, editing, and assembly of opinions for *CLSA Advisory Opinions 2022* were provided by Monsignor Michael A. Souckar, chair of the Publications Advisory Board, and Reverend Patrick M. Cooney, OSB, a member of the Publications Advisory Board. The topics addressed in the opinions reflect a variety of canonical issues and demonstrate the scope of canonical expertise andreflection by members of the Society. Editorial assistance was provided by the CLSA Executive Coordinator.

Recent past issues of *Roman Replies and CLSA Advisory Opinions* are available in the Society's online store. Past issues that are out-of-print are available electronically as PDFs on the CLSA website (clsa.org), and many are available as print-on-demand (POD) through Amazon.

The CLSA provides this series as a professional resource. Care should be taken in considering the relative weight of the materials found in this publication. The principles for canonical interpretation (*CIC* cc. 16-19 and *CCEO* cc. 1498-1501) serve as guides in considering the contents of this volume.

The editors are grateful to all who submitted texts to the three sections of this edition.

ROMAN REPLIES

INTRODUCTORY NOTE

The following is the editorial policy of *Roman Replies*. The policy, as well as the source of these materials, was first described in the 1984 edition and, with some modifications, has been in effect since that time.

Each year members of the Canon Law Society of America are invited to submit recent replies from the various dicasteries of the Holy See which might be of interest to the Society's members and the wider church. Judicial vicars, chancellors, vicars general, major superiors of institutes of consecrated life and societies of apostolic life in the United States, and professors of canon law are encouraged and asked to submit material for this important publication.

Contributions from members of the Society resident in other countries or members of other canon law societies are always most welcome. All contributors receive a complimentary copy of the volume.

Certain editorial principles determine the selection of documents for this publication. First, in general, entries which have already appeared in various canonical journals would not normally be repeated here. An exception is the publication of an official English translation of documents for which an unofficial translation already has been published. Second, documents which merely restate something published earlier with no added nuances or changes are not normally included. Third, documents that concern a matter not yet resolved by the Roman dicasteries are held for future publication in the hope that the entire matter may be fully reported when the question or controversy has been resolved. Finally, all details of names and places are changed to protect confidentiality, unless otherwise specified by the submitting individual.

A special note of thanks is extended to all those who have submitted texts, helped with translations, and otherwise contributed to this 2022 edition. It is our hope that this volume continues to be a service to all who work in the ministry of justice in the Church.

Contributions may be sent to:

Canon Law Society of America
415 Michigan Avenue NE, Suite 101
Washington, DC 20017-4502

OR via email to
ExecutiveCoordinator@clsa.org

Canons 220, 1077, 1099, 1457; and *Dignitas Connubii* Art. 251

Regarding the Application of Article 251 of *Dignitas Connubii* on the Imposition of a *Vetitum*

Inquiry to the Pontifical Council for Legislative Texts

I offer my thanks for your and the Council's several past provisions of clarifications of documents of the Holy See, especially the m.p. Mitis Iudex. *I would like to inquire about a particular provision of the Instruction Dignitas Connubii, that is, Article 251 on the imposition of a prohibition (*vetitum*), especially whether the text's statement of various causes is to be understood as taxative or illustrative. The paragraphs mention expressly only absolute impotence, permanent incapacity for marriage, deception (*dolus*), and simulation. May additional causes for imposition be admitted? This inquiry is motivated by the current efforts of a tribunal to resolve a petition for declaration of nullity of marriage by an unbaptized man with history of five civilly recognized marriages and four civil divorces. Two marriages were with the same woman. Two were entered before non-Catholic ministers of religion and three before civil magistrates. Three of the women have had marriages and divorces antecedently, including the petitioner's current civilly recognized spouse, who is the only Catholic involved. The petition seems to be tending toward affirmative answer according to c. 1099, error determining the will concerning the indissolubility of marriage, not expressly mentioned in Dignitas among the causes for imposition of a* vetitum. *Thus, there is also interest in guidance concerning canon 1077 that the local ordinary may impose a* vetitum. *Might a tribunal inform him, within the strictures of canons 220 and 1457 §1 et al.? And might the responses be permitted to be made known among other canonists?*

RESPONSUM

PONTIFICIUM CONSILIUM DE LEGUM TEXTIBUS

Città del Vaticano, 7 aprile 2022

Prot. N. xxxxx /2022

Reverendissimo Monsignore,

riscontro la Sua lettera del 19 marzo u.s., con la quale chiede il parere di questo Pontificio Consiglio riguardante l'art. 251 dell'Istr. Dignitas Connubii e il can. 1077 CIC sull'imposizione del vetitum.

Dopo aver studiato attentamente tale questione, mi premuro di comunicarLe quanto segue.

Il testo dell'art. 251 dell'Istr. Dignitas Connubii è meramente illustrativo e non tassativo. L'elenco delle cause per cui si può imporre il vetitum non è esaustivo e come sappiamo la decisione finale spetta al giudice, àhe può stabilire o no un vetitum, secondo il prudente discernimento in un caso concreto.

Lo scopo dei cann. 1077 1 e 1682 1 CIC e dell'art. 251 è quello di evitare la celebrazione di nuovi matrimoni nulli: è per questo che il tribunale o l'Ordinario del 'luogo, devono verificare se persiste o è stata superata la causa che ha portato la nullità del matrimonio.

Senza alcun dubbio si nuò 'applicare il vc it2i771 alPerrore deterà3iinante previsto nel can. 1099 CIC, se si ha la certezza che l'errore persiste e che determina la volontà, per cui un nuovo matrimonio sarebbe palesemente nullo.

Il can. 1077 stabilisce la competenza dell'Ordinario del luogo di vietare il matrimonio in un caso peculiare, per un tempo determinato, per una causa grave e fin tanto che questa perduri. Questo divieto riguarda sia il matrimonio che si vuole celebrare per la prima volta che le nuove nozze dopo la morte di uno dei coniugi o dopo aver ricevuto la sentenza che dichiara la nullità del precedente matrimonio emessa dâ tribunale ecclesiastico competente (cf. can. 1682 1 CIC).

Nel caso di nuove nozze dopo una sentenza che dichiara la nullità del matrimonio, il tribunale che ha giudicato la causa può informare l'Ordinario del luogo riguardo al motivo che ha motivato l'imposizione del vetitum e se questo può essere tolto dall'Ordinario o dal tribunale stesso.

Nella speranza di aver fornito utili considerazioni, colgo l'occasione per confermarmi,

della Signoria Vostra Rev.ma dev.mo in Domino

✠ /s/ Presidente	✠ /s/ Segretario

****

Unofficial Translation (by Recipient)

PONTIFICAL COUNCIL FOR LEGISLATIVE TEXTS

Vatican City, 7 April 2022

Prot. N. xxxxx /2022

Most Reverend Monsignor,

I refer to your letter of 19 March u.s., with which you ask for the opinion of this Pontifical Council regarding article 251 of the Instruction *Dignitas connubii* and canon 1077 *CIC* on the imposition of *vetitum.*

Having studied this matter carefully, I am taking care to inform you of the following:

The text of article 251 of the Instruction *Dignitas connubii* is merely illustrative and not exhaustive. The list of cases for which *vetitum* can be imposed is not exhaustive, and as we know the final decision is up to the judge, who can establish or not a *vetitum,* according to prudent discernment in the concrete case.

The purpose of canons 1077 §1 and 1682 §1 *CIC* and article 251 is to avoid the celebration of new null marriages. This is why the tribunal or the Ordinary of the place is to verify if the cause that led to the nullity of the marriage persists or has been overcome.

Without any doubt there would be the new act to apply the *vetitum* to the *error determinans* mentioned in canon 1099 *CIC*, if one is certain that the error persists and that it determines the will, so that a new marriage would be manifestly null and void.

The canon 1077 establishes the competence of the Ordinary of the place to prohibit marriage in a particular case, for a specific time, for a serious cause and as long as this persists. This prohibition concerns both a marriage to be celebrated for the first time and a new marriage after the death of one of the spouses or after receiving the sentence declaring the nullity of the previous marriage issued by the competent ecclesiastical tribunal (see canon 1682 §1 *CIC*).

In the case of new marriage after a sentence declaring the nullity of the marriage, the court that judged the case may inform the Ordinary of the place about the reason that motivated the imposition of the *vetitum* and whether this would be removed by the Ordinary or by the court itself.

In the hope of having provided useful considerations, I take this opportunity to assure you, Most Reverend Sir, as most devoted in the Lord.

/s/ — President

/s/ — Secretary

CANONS 587 §2; 624 §1; AND 627 §1

REGARDING CHANGES IN THE CONSTITUTION OF A RELIGIOUS INSTITUTE AND REQUEST FOR IMMEDIATE IMPLEMENTATION

A Superior General notified the Congregation for Institutes of Consecrated Life of the need to the institute's constitution to accommodate the decreasing number and aging of members fourteen months prior to the next chapter. She requested preliminary approval of the changes to be voted on by the chapter and effective for elections at the same chapter. The Archbishop Secretary of the CICLSAL acknowledged and requested the Superior General resend the request once the changes had been approved by the chapter. The correspondence between the Superior General and the CICLSAL also addressed the future need for a Commissary when the institute was no longer able to provide its canonical governance. Following the vote of the chapter on the proposed changes, the Superior General forwarded the results to CICLSAL requesting approval for immediate implementation of the changes. The approval was granted and sent to the Superior General within 4 hours. The correspondence follows.

November 17, 2020

His Eminence
Prefect
Congregation for Institutes of Consecrated Life
and Societies of Apostolic Life
00120 Vatican City

Your Eminence:

We, the Sisters of [ ] are a pontifical congregation with 92 members as of the date of this letter. Our members range from 53 to 100 years of age, and our median age is 81. Our last new member professed vows in the year 2000.

My term of office and that of my Council members ends on June 30, 2022. During the current six-year leadership term, which began in 2016, two of the four Council members have resigned for health reasons, one in August 2019 and one in August 2020. Per the requirements of our Constitutions, we did appoint a replacement after the first resignation. To date, we have not been able to identify a replacement Councilor for the second resignation.

We met with our sisters to consider options for our future. Sixty six of our ninety-two members participated in a meeting in September. (The twenty-six who did not participate are elderly and in declining health; seventeen are receiving skilled nursing care.) At that meeting, all present supported requesting approval for the following changes to our Constitutions:

- Length of term for the Superior General and Councilors from six years to three years
- Possibility of re-election of the present Superior General and Councilors, not to exceed two successive terms
- Reduction of the number of Councilors

Given our sisters' support of requesting the above changes and our difficulty in identifying someone to fill the vacancy, we plan to experiment with having three councilors for the remaining months of the current tern1.

I hereby respectfully request preliminary approval of the above changes so that they can be voted upon by the Chapter Members in 2022 and become effective for that Chapter. I am enclosing a copy of our Constitutions as well as a copy the relevant paragraphs with a draft of the requested changes.

If you need further information, I can be reached at the address on this letterhead or by email at

Thank you for your consideration of this request. I will look forward to receiving your response.

Sincerely,

/s/

Superior General

Enclosures: Constitutions
Relevant Paragraphs with Draft of Suggested Changes

****

Congregation for Institutes of Consecrated Life
and Societies of Apostolic Life

Prot. n. xxx/2004

Vatican City, January 12, 2021

Dear Sr. [Name]:

Your letter of November 17 has been received in this office of the Congregation for Institutes of Consecrated Life and Societies of Apostolic Life. In that letter you presented desired modifications to the Constitutions which were supported by all the Sisters and will be voted during the Chapter to be held in 2022.

We have taken note that you will remain with three councillors for the remaining months of the current term of the general council. Concerning the modifications to the Constitutions once they have been voted on and approved by 2/3 of the chapter members, we ask that you resend the request so that it can be granted.

We are pleased to note that, you have already established a civil organizational structure of collaborative governance with another institute. We ask that you now tend to the ecclesial and canonical requirements. This Dicastery suggests that you seriously study the possibility of a fusion with another Institute or the naming of a Superior General of another Institute, or a competent, qualified religious, to serve as a Pontifical Commissary for your Institute. In either case, after having received your input, the approval and nomination of the latter would be the responsibility of this Congregation for Institutes of Consecrated Life and Societies of Apostolic Life.

I take this opportunity to offer my prayerful support to you and all the sisters as you discern the future of the Congregation.

Sincerely in Christ,

/s/
Archbishop Secretary

****

March 2, 2021

Most Rev. [ ] Archbishop Secretary
Congregation for Institutes of Consecrated Life
and Societies of Apostolic Life
00120 Vatican City

Dear Archbishop [ ]:

Thank you for your January 12, 2021 response to our institute's request for modifications to our Constitutions. We are grateful for your understanding of our situation and for your willingness to assist us.

When the General Chapter convenes (currently scheduled for March 25-30, 2022), the Chapter Members will vote on the proposed modifications. We will then resend the request to your office for final approval.

We are working toward identifying a competent, qualified religious who could serve as our Superior General when we no longer have a sister of our own to fulfill this responsibility. We do understand that the approval of this person is the responsibility of the Congregation for Institutes of Consecrated Life and Societies of Apostolic Life.

Once again, please accept my appreciation for your assistance to us and for your important service to religious institutes throughout the world.

Sincerely,

/s/

Sister [Name]
Superior General

****

Congregation for Institutes of Consecrated Life
and Societies of Apostolic Life

Prot. n. xxx/2004

Vatican City, March 29, 2021

Dear Sr. [Name]:

Thank you for your letter of March 2 which has been received in this office of the *Congregation for Institutes of Consecrated Life and Societies of Apostolic Life.*

We noted your desire to work toward identifying a competent, qualified religious who could assist the leadership of the institute when you no longer have sisters of your own to fulfil the responsibility and we look forward to receiving updates on the situation of the institute, prior to or following the General Chapter currently scheduled for March 2022. Please know that the Dicastery is available to assist you as needed.

May the Holy Spirit inspire and guide you and all the members of the forthcoming General Chapter. May the event be marked by fraternal dialogue and mutual acceptance, with attention to the signs of the times and a shared reflection on your *founding charism,* so as to give new impetus to the mission of the Institute.

I entrust you to the maternal intercession of the Blessed Virgin and I assure you of my prayer and my blessing during these most unprecedented times of the COVID-19 pandemic.

Sincerely in Christ,
/s/
Archbishop Secretary

****

Congregation for Institutes of Consecrated Life
and Societies of Apostolic Life

Prot. n. xxx/2004

Vatican City, March 26, 2022

Dear Sr. [Name]:

This office has received your email of March 24 requesting modifications to the Constitutions that will be effective immediately in order to proceed with elections during the current general chapter.

As more than 2/3 of the members have voted the proposed changes, this dicastery grants approval in conformity with the request for the modification of articles 33.1 and 34.1 of the Constitutions as noted below.

33.1 --To be eligible for the office of superior general a sister must be thirty-five years of age and perpetually professed at least seven years. Her term of office is three years. Having completed her term of office she may be immediately re-elected to the office of superior general or to the council, not to exceed two terms.

34.1 - To be eligible for the office of general councilor a sister must be perpetually professed at least three years. The members of the general council are elected for a term of three years and are eligible for immediate re-election, not to exceed two terms. The number of councilors will be at least two and no more than four.

I take this opportunity to offer my prayerful support to you and all the members of the General Chapter.

Sincerely in Christ,

/s/

Secretary

/s/ Sr. []

Undersecretary

CANON 587

REGARDING EXTENSION OF TERM OF OFFICE FOR INTERIM SUPERIOR GENERAL FOLLOWING DEATH OF SUPERIOR GENERAL

Following the death of a Superior General, the Interim Superior General took office in accord with the institute's constitutions. The Superior General's death occurred slightly more than a year prior to the next scheduled general chapter. According to the constitutions, a chapter of elections was to take place to elect a new Superior General if the vacancy in the office occurred more than a year prior to a scheduled general chapter. The Interim Superior General notified the Congregation for Institutes of Consecrated Life of the Superior General's death and requested a dispensation from the constitutions to permit the current interim Superior General and council to remain in office until the next scheduled general chapter. The Congregation for Institutes of Consecrated Life sent prayerful condolences on the death of the Superior General and, considering the aging members and the institute's discernment about future canonical governance, approved the request within three days. The correspondence follows.

Congregation for Institutes of Consecrated Life Prot. n. xxx/2022
and Societies of Apostolic Life

Vatican City, May 23, 2022

Dear Sr. [Name]:

Your letter of May 5 has been received in this dicastery. Please accept the condolences and prayers of our staff on the passing of your general superior, Sr. [Name]. May she receive the reward of her life dedicated to Christ and the service of the Church, may she also intercede for each member during these challenging times.

We have noted your request for a dispensation from your Constitutions to enable the current interim leadership: interim general superior and two general councillors, to remain in office until the May 2023 chapter. In light of the current congregational status and need for discernment for future governance, we accept and approve the above request.

I take this opportunity to cordially greet you in the Lord Jesus and to assure all the members of the Congregation of my prayer during the Easter Season of Resurrection.

Sincerely in Christ,

/s/ /s/ Sr. []
Secretary *Undersecretary*

Canon 1295

Regarding A Bishop's Request that Parishes Share in Funding the Monetary Obligation Arising from the Settlement of Sexual Abuse Cases

A pastor of three parishes in a U.S. diocese objected to the imposition of a tax on all parishes to help pay off the debt incurred as a result of the diocese having filed bankruptcy in the wake of its sexual abuse lawsuits. The pastor sought recourse to the Congregation for Clergy in 2018 and then to the Apostolic Signatura in 2019. Following are selections from the correspondence from the case.

Prefect Congregation for the Clergy
c/o His Eminence [Name]

Piazza Pio XII 3
00193 Rome, Italy
FAX 011.[. . .]

30July 2018

Your Eminence,

I send this request to the Congregation for Clergy with the request for your intervention and our seeking recourse against the demand of our Bishop [Name] from the Diocese of [Diocese] who is stipulating that we as parishes take on $x million of the $xx million bankruptcy settlement that is filed against the diocese.

I was assigned as pastor in 2017 with financial responsibility and oversight (enclosed). Unfortunately, the main parish of St. [Name]'s had incurred financial limitations in meeting the Diocesan Appeal and Cathedradicum Tax and owes in excess of $88,000.00 from past years. As I stated in the June 5, 2018 reply (enclosed) I in my duties as pastor, in consultation with designated council members, find it would be irresponsible and negligent to commit to adding the $30,534.00 (revised from $36,800.00) which is now (cf. July 23, 2018 email from Bishop [Name]) to be as a promissory note with 4% interest. There are additionally terms contained within the contract that are burdensome and are devoid of a relationship that should relate to parish communities in appreciation of their generosity rather than stipulate minute details by exacting minute penalties by making donations compulsory.

The promissory note interest is problematic, especially on these funds. The funds from which these loans are being borrowed are parish savings held at the Capital Asset Support Corporation (CASC) and administered by the Dioceses. The parishes who have funds in the CASC receive 1.5% interest while the diocese retains 2.5% of the interest. The financial arrangement of this is unsupportable. It is the juridic person of the Diocese of [Diocese] that is named in the litigation, not the juridic person of the parishes. As U.S. Bankruptcy Court filings indicate the Diocese is the subject of the lawsuit and therefore should be assuming the indebtedness and interest on the loan, rather than benefiting from passing the debt to the parishes and capitalizing on over $2 million from parishes over the course of 15 years.

I would further plead with you for your intervention by referencing Canon 1295. The rural nature of these communities and the agricultural risks that they regularly incur have a continuous impact upon their viability and ability to provide donations. The demand of taking on this burden will worsen the patrimonial condition of the juridic persons of the communities in this assignment. This past year alone these communities and others throughout the diocese have incurred many natural disasters. We experienced drought and fire last year followed by a disastrous winter with 8-foot snow drifts and then came record flooding from the spring run-off.

I have enclosed my good faith efforts to encourage the people of the parish to participate in financially helping defray the cost of this lawsuit against the diocese to the degree they can. I also enclose letters where I offered recommendation to the diocese that I felt would be productive.

I would ask for your consideration in issuing an injunction on these matters to protect the juridic persons of the parishes of our diocese.

Sincerely in Christ,

Rev. Father [Name], JCL

****

From the Vatican, 15 February 2019

CONGREGATIO
PRO CLERICIS

Prot. N. 2019 0584

Reverend [Name]
Saint [ ] Parish
Post Office Box xxx
City, Sate Zip
UNITED STATES OF AMERICA

Dear Reverend Father,

I write in response to your letter of 25 January last, requesting reconsideration of this Dicastery's rejection of your petition for hierarchical recourse against the dispositions of His Excellency, the Bishop of [Diocese] concerning the promissory note that you claim was imposed on St [ ]'s Parish.

As previously explained, the promissory note regarding your parish bears your signature as the juridic representative of the parish (cf. can. 532), agreeing to the terms of the note. This makes it difficult for this Congregation to accept your petition as someone with aggrieved status under canon 1737 §1.

Having examined your documentation of the various pressures that were brought to bear on this situation by the Ordinary, the Dicastery would note that your arguments stem largely from American civil law, which is not the juridical system employed in hierarchical recourse. Nevertheless, a canonical approach to this question may be found in canon 125, which refers to juridic acts placed out of grave fear. Inasmuch as you were shown to have demonstrated a vigorous resistance to the Ordinary's pressure, only agreeing to sign at the end of a lengthy and somewhat heated dialogue, the promissory note as a juridic act is valid (cf. can. 125 §2).

With the juridic act of signing the promissory note in place, the Congregation is simply unable to consider you or St [ ]'s Parish aggrieved, and therefore, cannot accept the petition. Thus, per article 137 §1 of the *General Regulations of the Roman Curia,* your request for reconsideration must be rejected.

With sentiments of esteem and respect, I am,

Sincerely yours in Christ,

/s/

Prefect

/s/

Secretary

****

18 July 2019

Prot. n. xxxxx/19 CA

Reverend Father,

Having received and studied your recourse of 7 February 2019, the undersigned Secretary of the Apostolic Signatura has issued the enclosed decree rejecting the recourse *in limine.* because of evident lack of any foundation (enclosure A). The competence of the Supreme Tribunal in these matters is limited to questions of alleged violations of the law.

While you do have the right to have recourse to the *Congresso* of the Apostolic Signatura against this decision, within the peremptory time limit of ten days from the receipt of this letter, you should first consider carefully the utility of doing so, in light of the reasons given in the decree. Enclosed please find for your consideration an information sheet concerning contentious-administrative recourse to the Apostolic Signatura (enclosure B)

If you decide to challenge this decree for founded reasons, you must:

1. Make your recourse within the peremptory time limit of 10 days from your reception of this decree, indicating at least in a summary manner the specific reasons for challenging the decree (cf. artt. 28, §1 and 76, §3 *Legis propriae* of the Apostolic Signatura):

2. Submit within the peremptory time limit of 30 days from the reception of this decree the initial deposit of € 1550 (cf. Information sheet, n. 6) through the Apostolic Nunciature in Washington D.C. This can be done by sending a certified check in the amount of € 1550 payable to *Supremo Tribunale della Segnatura Apostolica* as a deposit for the expenses of the case:

Father [Name]
Parish Priest
Church of St. [ ]
P.O. Box xxx
City, State (USA)

(with three enclosures)

3. You must choose a procurator-advocate from the attached list (enclosure C) within 40 days from the reception of this decree, and, after he or she has agreed to represent you, send here a mandate appointing that person to do so.

Sincerely yours in Christ.

+ /s/

Secretary

****

SUPREMUM SIGNATURAE
APOSTOLICAE TRIBUNAL

PALAZZO DELL CANCELLARIA
00120 CITTA DEL VATICANO

Prot. n. xxxx/19 CA
[DIOCESE]
Rescissio l lis contractus
(Rev.dus M. [Name] - Congregatio pro Clericis)

DECRETUM

Rev.dus [Name] decreto Exe.mi Episcopi diei 1 iulii 2017 parochus paroeciarum [Parish 1] in pago v.d. [*City*], [Parish 2] in pago v.d. [*City*] et [Parish 3] in pago v.d. [*City*] nominatus est.

Die 25 maii 2018 Exc.mus Episcopus v.d. "commitment letters" ad parochos dioecesis misit, ut adnexum contractum de contributione ad expensas pacificae compositionis (v.d. *settlement)* inter Dioecesim [Diocese] et assertas victimas delicti contra sextum decalogi praeceptum subscriberent.

Die 20 iunii 2018 Exc.mus Episcopus Rev.dum [Name] certiorem fecit maiorem partem paroeciarum iam invitationem secutam esse, sed eidem facultatem patere subscriptionem recusare. Die 20 iulii 2018 Rev.dus [Name] respondit paroecias suas ob calamitates naturales contractum subscribere non posse.

Litteris diei 23 iulii 2018 Exc.mus Episcopus Rev.dum [Name] et nonnullos alios parochos certiores fecit de ab iis omissa subscriptione, et iterum facsimile v.d. *Promissmy Note* adnexit.

Litteris diei 30 iulii 2018 Rev.dus [Name] se apud Congregationem pro Clericis de adhortatione Exc.mi Episcopi eonquestus est.

Colloquio die 31 iulii 2018 apud advocatum eivilem inter Exc.mum Episcopum, Rev.dum [Name], et quattuor paroecianos peracto, Rev.dus [Name] die 2 augusti 2018 et Exc.mus Episcopus die 7 augusti 2018 v.d. *Promissory Note* nomine paroeciae

[Parish 1] et D.nus [Name] utpote Praeses, scilicet v.d. *Diocese of*[Diocese] *Juridic Persons Capital Asset Support Corporation,* die 28 augusti 2018 subsignaverunt.

Voto Exc.mi Episcopi recepto Congregatio die 7 ianuarii 2019 petitionem Rev.di [Name] adversus assertam impositionem tributi a paroecia S. [Parish 1]

dioecesi solvendi et petitionem novae audientiae die 15 februarii 2019 reiecit.

Quam adversus responsionem negativam Rev.dus [Name] iam die 7 februarii 2019 ad Supremum Signaturae Apostolicae Tribunal provocaverat.

Actis a Congregatione pro examine praeliminari exquisitis iisque receptis ac rimatis,

SUPREMUM SIGNATURAE APOSTOLICAE TRIBUNAL

Re sedulo examini subiecta;

De praesupposito apud Congregationem perpenso quod:

- Litteris diei 20 iunii 2018 Exc.mus Episcopus Rev.do [Name] in memoriam revocavit, maiorem partem parochorum v.d. *Promissori Note* iam accepisse;

- Iisdem litteris Exc.mus Episcopus in facultate Rev.di Recurrentis v.d. *Promissory Note* respuendi institit;

- Nec litteris die 23 iulii 2018 ope cursus electronici missis Exc.mus Episcopus Rev.do Recurrenti quid praecepit, sed tantum opera persuasionis prosecutus est;

- Die 31 iulii 2018 apud officium advocati civilis solummodo colloquium inter Exc.mum Episcopum, Advocatum civilem Dioecesis, Rev.dum [Name] et nonnullos paroecianos peractum est quo Exc.mus Episcopus cum Rev.do [Name] communicavit, iam 90 paroecias contribuisse:

Cum nullus actus administrativus singularis, exempli gratia decretum vel praeceptum, sed tantum invitatio penes Congregationem impugnata fuerit;

De assertis violationibus legis in decemendo, perpenso quod:

- Sermo de violatione can. 1263 fieri nequit, quia paroeciae cum Dioecesi [Diocese] systemate vulgo dicto *corporation sole* connexae sunt;

- Ad tuenda bona paroeciarum Exe.mus Episcopus consensum scriptum parochorum expetiit, servata facultate consensum denegandi;

- Exc.mus Episcopus litteris diei 20 iunii 2018 expressis verbis asseruit non agi de tributo, quod argumentum Congregatio ergo merito accepit;

- In v.d. *Promissory Note* claris verbis indicatum est non agi de donatione, sed de

- mutuo dein die 1 septembris 2018 concesso et intra diem 31 augusti 2033 restituendo;

Cum proinde Congregatio recursum hierarchicum ob defectum praesuppositi scilicet actus administrativi singularis recte reiecerit nec adsit fumus boni iuris ob assertam violationem legis;

Praetermissis aliis quoque ad rem forte animadvertendis;

Audito Rev.do Promotore Iustitiae Substituto;

Vi art. 76, § 1, n. 3 *Legis propriae* H.S.T.,

decrevit:

Recursum in limine reiciendum esse et facto reici, utpote indubie atque evidenter quovis fundamento carentem.

Adversus hoc decretum datur recursus ad Congressum intra peremptorium decem dierum terminum ab eodem recepto (cf. art. 76, § 3 *Legis propriae* H.S.T.).

Et notificetur omnibus, quorum interest, ad omnes iuris effectus.

Datum Romae, e Sede Supremi Signaturae Apostolicae Tribunalis, die 18 iulii 2019.

+/s/
Episcopus tit. Fundanus
Secretarius

/s/
vices Notarii gerens

****

Unofficial Translation

DECREE

Reverend [Name], by decree of his Excellency the bishop, was named Pastor on July 1, 2017, of [Parish 1] in [city], [Parish 2] in [city], and [Parish 3] in [city].

On May 25, 2018, his Excellency the Bishop sent commitment letters to the pastors of the diocese so they could sign the attached contract on contributions to the expenses of peaceful settlement between the Diocese and alleged victims of delicts against the Six Commandment of the Decalogue.

On June 20, 2018, the Bishop informed Reverend [Name] that the majority of the parishes had followed the invitation, but he was open to the possibility of refusing to sign. On July 20, 2018, Reverend [Name] replied that he could not subscribe to the contract due to natural calamities.

And a letter dated July 23, 2018, the Bishop informed Reverend [Name] and some other pastors of the omission of their signatures, and again attached a facsimile of the promissory note.

In a letter dated July 30, 2018, Reverend [Name] appealed to the Congregation for the Clergy about the exhortation of the Bishop.

After a meeting with the civil lawyers on July 31, 2018, between the Bishop, Reverend [Name], and four parishioners, Reverend [Name] on August 2, 2018, and his Excellency the Bishop on August 7, 2018, signed the promissory note in the name of [Parish 1], and Mr. [Name] as president of the diocese *Juridic Persons Capital Asset Support Corporation* on August 28, 2018.

Having received the votum of his Excellency the Bishop, on January 7, 2019, the Congregation rejected the petition of Reverend [Name] against the alleged imposition of a tax on the [Parish 1] and the request for a new hearing on February 15, 2019.

In the face of this negative response Reverend [Name] already had appealed on February 7, 2019, to the Supreme Tribunal of the Apostolic Signatura.

The acts of the Congregation were received and carefully examined for preliminary examination,

Supreme Tribunal of The Apostolic Signature

Subject to careful examination;

Regarding the presupposition of the Congregation, I consider that:

- In a letter dated June 20, 2018, the Bishop in memory recalled to Reverend [Name] that he had already received the promissory note from a majority of the pastors;
- In the same letter the bishop insisted on rejecting the Reverend Appellant's promissory note;
- Neither in the letter of July 23, 2018, sent with the help of electronic causes, did the bishop instruct the Reverend Appellant, but he only continued the work of persuasion;
- On July 31, 2018, at the office of the civil lawyer a conference was held between the bishop, the civil attorney for the diocese, Reverend [Name], and some parishioners in which the Bishop with Reverend [Name] shared that already 90 parishes had contributed;

Since no singular administrative act, for example a decree or precept, but only an invitation has been challenged to the Congregation;

In determining the alleged violations of the law, I consider that:

- To talk about a violation of Canon 1263 is not possible, because the parishes are connected with the Diocese system commonly called corporation sole;:

- To protect the goods of the parishes, the Bishop sought written consent of the parishioners, preserving the possibility of denying consent;

- The Bishop asserted in words expressed in the letter dated June 20, 2018, that it was not about the tax, which argument the Congregation therefore accepted on its merits;

- In the promissory note is clearly stated it is not to be a donation, but a loan granted on September 1, 2018, and to be repaid by August 31, 2033;

Since, therefore, the Congregation correctly rejected the hierarchical recourse due to the failure of the presupposed singular administrative act, and there is no evidence of *boni iuris* due to the alleged violation of the law;

Passing over others also to take notice of the matter;

At the hearing of the Rev. Promoter of Justice Substitute;

By virtue of art. 76, § 1, n. 3 *Legis propriae* of this Supreme Tribunal,

I decree:

The recourse must be rejected at the threshold (*in limine*), and it was rejected as a matter of fact, as it undoubtedly and evidently lacks any foundation.

Faced with this decree, recourse must be given to the *Congressum* within a peremptory term of ten days from receipt of the same (cf. art. 76, § 3 *Legis propriae* of this Supreme Tribunal).

And it will be notified to all those who are interested, for all legal effects.

Given at Rome, from the seat of the Supreme Tribunal of the Apostolic Signatura, on July 18, 2019.

TRADITIONIS CUSTODES ART. 3 §2

REGARDING A REQUEST FOR DISPENSATION

A bishop requested clarification from the Congregation for Divine Worship and Discipline of the Sacraments with regard to the application of the motu proprio Traditionis Custodes *in a specific situation.*

January 27, 2022
Most Reverend . . . Prefect
The Congregation for Divine Worship and the Discipline of the Sacraments
Palazzo delle Congregazioni 00193 Roma
Piazza Pio XII, 10

Your Excellency,

In the [Diocese], there exists a small contingency that has requested that the celebration of the Eucharist using the *Missale Romanum (Editio typica* 1962). Only one priest in the Archdiocese has been granted the faculty to do so and a personal parish for this group of the faithful does not exist.

The faithful gather in Saint [ ] Catholic Church, where my delegate is canonically assigned, and he celebrates Mass in Latin once on Sunday, as well as once on the First Friday and the First Saturday of each month. These Masses, though celebrated in a parochial church, are a concession limited to this group and is not part of the ordinary life of the parish community. It is not included in the parish Mass schedule and the pastor of the parish, who celebrates the Mass in Latin, promotes and upholds the teachings of the Second Vatican Council and encourages those who attend the Tridentine Mass to do the same.

By continuing the Tridentine Mass in the current setting, the faithful requesting this Mass are being accommodated, while not overtaxing the pastor. Additionally, the only options for the use of a sacred space in the city of [City], other than a parochial church, would be a university chapel. In my opinion, this option poses the danger of encouraging the Tridentine Mass among young adults.

Therefore, as requested in *Traditionis custodes,* I hereby apply for a dispensation from Article 3, §2 of the *motu proprio* and request that the parochial church of Saint Timothy Catholic Church, located in the city of [City, State], be allowed for the celebration of the Eucharist, utilizing the *Missale Romanum* of 1962.

Sincerely yours in Christ,

Most Reverend [Bishop of Diocese]

CONGREGATIO DE CULTU DIVINO
ET DISCIPLINA SACRAMENTORUM

Prot. N. xxx/22

Vatican City, 28 February 2022

Your Excellency,

The Congregation received your letter of 27 January in which you ask for a dispensation from art. 3 §2 of the Motu proprio *Traditionis custodes* so that Mass according to the *Missale Romanum* of 1962 can be celebrated in the parish church of Saint [ ] in the city of [City, State].

After a careful study of the pastoral reasons Your Excellency has presented we now send you the decree by which the dispensation is granted for a period of two years. If, after this period of time, you wish to renew the permission then you will need to send us a *relatio* along with your request. This *relatio* should contain details of the number of participants at these Masses and it should also recount the steps which have been taken to lead the faithful who are attached to the antecedent liturgy towards the celebration of the liturgy according to the liturgical books reformed by decree of the Second Vatican Council, and which form the unique expression of the *lex orandi* of the Roman Rite.

We are grateful to Your Excellency for the steps you are taking to ensure the correct application of the Motu proprio *Traditionis custodes.*

With every good wish and kind regard, I am,

Fraternally yours in Christ,

ffi /s/

Prefect

(attachment)

CONGREGATIO DE CULTU DIVINO
ET DISCIPLINA SACRAMENTORUM

Prot. N. xxx/22

[DIOCESE]

Instante Excellentissimo [Bishop of Diocese], litteris die 27 mensis ianuarii 2022 datis, vigore facultatum peculiarium huic Congregationi a Summo Pontifice FRANCISCO tributarum, attentis expositis, licentiam celebrandi secundum Missale Romanum a sancto Ioanne XXIII anno 1962 promulgatum, in ecclesia parreciali Deo in honorem sancti [ ] dicata, in civitate [City], perlibenter concedimus, servatis semper de iure servandis.

Quae gratia *ad biennium* conceditur et, eo transacto, relatio de supradicta licentia ad hanc Congregationem trasmittatur.

Contrariis quibuslibet minime obstantibus.

Ex redibus Congregationis de Cultu Divino et Disciplina Sacramentorum, die 28 mensis februarii 2022.

-ffi /s/e

Prafectus

ffi /s/
Episcopus Subsecretarius

****

Unofficial Translation

[Diocese]

At the instance of His Excellency [Bishop of Diocese], in a letter dated January 27, 2022, with the strength of the special faculties given to this Congregation by the Supreme Pontiff FRANCIS, with careful consideration, permission to celebrate according to the Roman Missal promulgated by St. John XXIII in 1962, in the parish church Dedicated to God in honor of St. [ ], in the city of [City], we gladly grant, always observing the law.

This grace is granted for two years, and, at the end of that time, a report on the aforesaid license is sent to this Congregation.

Notwithstanding anything to the contrary.

From the returns of the Congregation for Divine Worship and the Discipline of the Sacraments, February 28, 2022.

/s/ Prefect and Bishop Subsecretary signatures

CCEO Canon 916 §5; *Dignitas Connubii* art. 16, §1

Competency of Latin Tribunals Extended to Eritrean Church in Canada

In June of 2022, the Apostolic Signatura expanded competency for Eritreans in Canada to the local Latin tribunals after receiving requests from officials of Latin tribunals.

SUPREMUM SIGNATURAE APOSTOLICAE TRIBUNAL

PALAZZO DELLA CANCELLERIA 00120 CITTA DEL VATICANO

Prot. n. xxx/22 SAT

Praehabitis variis instantiis apud hoc Supremum Tribunal porrectis, quibus officiales Tribunalium Latinorum in Canada prorogationem competentiae pro christifidelibus Ecclesiae Erythraeae domicilium in illo territorio habentibus petierunt, ita ut causa singula nullitatis matrimonii Foro Latino committeretur, potius quam apud Forum Erythraeum unicum iure competens definiretur,

SUPREMUM SIGNATURAE APOSTOLICAE TRIBUNAL

Re sedulo examini subiecta;

Prae oculis habito quod in praefato territorio exarchia quidem pro christifidelibus Ecclesiae Erythraeae nondum erecta est, et plures sunt Ordinarii loci alterius Ecclesiae sui iuris;

Viso quod, attentis a Dicasterio pro Ecclesiis Orientalibus in litteris diei 14 iunii 2022 expositis (cf. prot. n. 214/2015), Ordinarius loci alterius Ecclesiae sui iuris nondum designatus est (cf. can. 916, § 5 CCEO et art. 16, §1, n. 1 Instructionis *Dignitas connubii*);

Firmo manente art. 16, § 1, n. 2 praefatae Instructionis;

Audito Rev.mo Promotore Iustitiae deputato;

Vi artt. 194 et 198, n. 4 Const. Apost. *Praedicate Evangelium* necnon artt. 32 et 35, n. 3 *Legis propriae* qua hoc Supremum Tribunal regitur,

decrevit:

> Prorogandam esse et facto prorogari competentiam ita ut causae nullitatis matrimonii Erythraeae pertractari ac definiri queant apud illud tribunal Ecclesiae latinae in Canada quod competentia gauderet si partes essent Ecclesiae Latinae, done aliter provideatur.

Animadverso quod hisce in causis oportet Tribunal Ecclesiae latinae procedat iuxta legem processualem propriam, sed nullitas matrimonii definienda est secundum leges Ecclesiae Erythraeae (cf. art. 16, § 2 praefatae Instructionis).

Quod notificetur iis quorum interest ad omnes iuris effectus.

Datum Romae, apud sedem Supremi Signaturae Apostolicae Tribunalis, die 23 iunii 2022.

/s/
Praefectus

/s/
Secretarius

****

Unofficial Translation

Various instances were presented before the Supreme Tribunal in which the officials of the Latin Tribunals in Canada have requested an extension of competency for members of the Eritrean Christian Church who have domicile in that territory in such a way that a separate case of nullity of marriage could be committed to the Latin Forum, rather than in the case of the Eritrean Forum,

SUPREME TRIBUNAL OF THE APOSTOLIC SIGNATURA

The subject has been carefully examined

I should keep in mind that in the aforesaid territory an exarchy of the Eritrean Church has not yet been erected for the Christian faithful, and there are several local Ordinaries of another Church *sui iuris*;

Having seen that, after considering the letter set forth by the Dicastery for the Eastern Churches on 14 June 2022 (cf. prot. n. 214/2015), the local ordinary of another Church *sui iuris* has not yet been designated (cf. c. 91 §5 CCEO and art. 16, §1, n.1 of the Instruction *Dignitas connubii*);

By remaining firm in art. 16, §1, n. 2 of the aforementioned Instruction;

Having heard the Most Rev. Promoter of Justice, his deputy;

By virtue of artt. 194 and 198, n. 4. apost. const *Praedicate Evangelium* as well as artt. 32 and 35, n. 3 of the *Legis propriae* by which this Supreme Tribunal is governed,

It is decreed:

> The competence should be and is extended in such a way that the reasons for the nullity of the Eritrean marriage may be discussed and determined at that tribunal of the Latin Church in Canada that would enjoy competence if they were part of the Latin Church, otherwise it is to be provided.

I observe that in these cases the tribunal of the Latin Church must proceed according to its own procedural law, but the nullity of the marriage must be determined according to the laws of the Eritrean Church (cf. art. 16, §2 of the aforementioned Instruction).

This is to be notified to all interested parties to the effect of law.

Given in Rome, at the seat of the Supreme Tribunal Apostolic Signatura, 23 June 2022.

/s/
Praefectus

/s/
Secretarius

OTHER VATICAN DOCUMENTS

Rescriptum ex Audientia SS.mi

The Supreme Pontiff Francis graciously affirms the prayers of the Congregation for the Doctrine of the Faith, such as the *Norms on more grave delicts reserved to the same Congregation*, the Apostolic Letter Motu Proprio under the inscription "*Sacramentorum Sanctitatis Tutela*" promulgated by St. John Paul II on April 30, 2001 and revised by the Supreme Pontiff Benedict XVI on May 21, 2010, will be edited according to the new edition that follows, ordering at the same time that they will come into force together with this Rescript on December 8, 2021 and will be made public in the newspaper *L'Osservatore Romano* and then be published in the *Acta Apostolica Sedis*, the official commentary of the same, anything to the contrary, even worthy of mention, notwithstanding.

October 11, 2021.

/s/
Praefectus

✠ /s/
Archiepiscopus tit. Caeretanus
a Secretis

****

Norms Regarding Delicts Reserved to the Congregation for the Doctrine of the Faith

Part One: Substantive Norms

Art. 1

§1 The Congregation for the Doctrine of the Faith, according to art. 52 of the Apostolic Constitution *Pastor bonus*, judges delicts against the faith, in accordance with art. 2 §2, and also the more grave delicts committed against morals and in the celebration of the sacraments and, whenever necessary, proceeds to declare or impose canonical sanctions according to the norm of both common and proper law, with due regard for the competence of the Apostolic Penitentiary and in keeping with the *Agendi ratio in doctrinarum examine*.

§2 With regard to the delicts mentioned above in §1, the Congregation for the Doctrine of the Faith, by prior mandate of the Roman Pontiff, may judge Cardinals, Patriarchs, Legates of the Apostolic See, Bishops, as well as other physical persons mentioned in can. 1405 §3 of the Code of Canon Law (=*CIC*), and in can. 1061 of the Code of Canons of the Eastern Churches (=*CCEO*).

§3 The Congregation for the Doctrine of the Faith judges the reserved delicts mentioned in §1 according to the following norms.

Art. 2

§1 The delicts against the faith mentioned in art. 1 are heresy, apostasy, and schism according to the norm of cann. 751 and 1364 *CIC*, and cann. 1436 and 1437 *CCEO*.

§2 In the above-mentioned cases referred to in §1, it pertains to the Ordinary or Hierarch, according to the norm of law, to undertake either a judicial trial in the first instance or an extrajudicial process concluding with a decree, with due regard for the right of appeal or of recourse to the Congregation for the Doctrine of the Faith.

§3 In the above-mentioned cases referred to in §1, it pertains to the Ordinary or Hierarch, according to the norm of law, to remit the *latae sententiae* excommunication or major excommunication, respectively, in the external forum.

Art. 3

§1 The more grave delicts against the sanctity of the most Holy Sacrifice and Sacrament of the Eucharist reserved to the Congregation for the Doctrine of the Faith for judgment are:

1° the taking or retaining for a sacrilegious purpose or the throwing away of the consecrated species, as mentioned in can. 1382 §1 *CIC* and in can. 1442 *CCEO*;

2° attempting the liturgical action of the Eucharistic Sacrifice as mentioned in can. 1379 §1, 1° *CIC*;

3° the simulation of the liturgical action of the Eucharistic Sacrifice, as mentioned can. 1379 §5 *CIC* and in can. 1443 *CCEO*;

4° the concelebration of the Eucharistic Sacrifice prohibited according to the norm of can. 908 *CIC* and can. 702 *CCEO*, as mentioned in can. 1381 *CIC* and in can. 1440 *CCEO*, with ministers of ecclesial communities which do not have apostolic succession and do not acknowledge the sacramental dignity of priestly ordination.

§2 Also reserved to the Congregation for the Doctrine of the Faith is the delict which consists in the consecration for a sacrilegious purpose of one matter without the other or even of both, either within or outside of the Eucharistic celebration, which is mentioned in can. 1382 §2 *CIC*.

Art. 4

§1 The more grave delicts against the sanctity of the Sacrament of Penance reserved to the judgment of the Congregation for the Doctrine of the Faith are:

1° the absolution of an accomplice in a sin against the sixth commandment of the Decalogue, mentioned in can. 1384 *CIC* and in can. 1457 *CCEO*;

2° the attempted sacramental absolution or the prohibited hearing of confession, mentioned in can. 1379 § 1, 2° *CIC*;

3° simulated sacramental absolution, as mentioned in can. 1379 §5 *CIC* and in can. 1443 *CCEO*;

4° the solicitation to a sin against the sixth commandment of the Decalogue in the act, on the occasion, or under the pretext of confession, as mentioned in can. 1385 *CIC* and in can. 1458 *CCEO*, if it is directed to sinning with the confessor himself;

5° the direct and indirect violation of the sacramental seal, as mentioned in can. 1386 §1 *CIC* and in can. 1456 §1 *CCEO*;

6° the recording, made by any technical means whatsoever, or the malicious diffusion through any form of communications media, of what is said in sacramental confession, whether actual or simulated, by the confessor or the penitent, as mentioned in can. 1386 §3 *CIC*.

§2 In the cases concerning the delicts mentioned in §1, it is not permitted for anyone to indicate the name of the accuser or the penitent either to the accused or to his or her patron, unless the one making the accusation or the penitent has expressly consented; the question of the credibility of the accuser is to be considered attentively; and any danger of violating the sacramental seal is to be altogether avoided, taking care, however, that the right of defense of the accused remains intact.

Art. 5

The more grave delict of the attempted sacred ordination of a woman is also reserved to the Congregation for the Doctrine of the Faith:

1° if the one who attempts to confer sacred ordination or the woman who attempts to receive sacred ordination are members of the Christian faithful subject to the *CIC*, they shall incur excommunication *latae sententiae*, the remission of which is reserved to the Apostolic See according to the norm of can. 1379 §3 *CIC*;

2° if the one who attempts to confer sacred ordination on a woman or the woman who attempts to receive sacred ordination are members of the Christian faithful subject to the *CCEO*, they are to be punished by a major excommunication, the remission of which is reserved to the Apostolic See.

Art. 6

The more grave delicts against morals which are reserved to the judgment of the Congregation for the Doctrine of the Faith are:

1° the delict against the sixth commandment of the Decalogue committed by a cleric with a minor below the age of eighteen years or with a person who habitually has the imperfect use of reason; ignorance or error on the part of the cleric regarding the age of the minor does not constitute an extenuating or exonerating circumstance;

2° the acquisition, possession, exhibition, or distribution, for purposes of sexual gratification or profit, of pornographic images of minors under the age of eighteen years, in any manner and by any means whatsoever, by a cleric.

Art. 7

Whoever commits the delicts mentioned in artt. 2-6, besides what is established for individual delicts in the *CIC* and in the *CCEO,* as well as in these present Norms, is to be punished, as the case warrants, with a just penalty according to the gravity of the crime; if committed by a cleric, he may also be punished by dismissal or deposition from the clerical state.

Art. 8

§1 Criminal action concerning delicts reserved to the Congregation for the Doctrine of the Faith is extinguished by prescription after twenty years.

§2 Prescription runs according to the norm of can. 1362 §2 *CIC* and can. 1152 §3 *CCEO*. However, in the case of the delict mentioned in art. 6 n. 1, prescription begins on the day the minor reaches the age of eighteen.

§3 The Congregation for the Doctrine of the Faith has the right to derogate from prescription for all individual cases of reserved delicts, even if they regard delicts committed prior to the coming into force of the present Norms.

Part Two: Procedural Norms

Title One: Concerning the Competence of the Tribunal

Art. 9

§1 The Congregation for the Doctrine of the Faith is the Supreme Apostolic Tribunal for the Latin Church as well as the Eastern Catholic Churches, for the judgment of the delicts defined in the preceding articles.

§2 This Supreme Tribunal, only in conjunction with the delicts reserved to it, also judges other delicts for which a defendant is accused by reason of connection of person and of complicity in a delict.

§3 Delicts reserved to this Supreme Tribunal are to be tried in a judicial process or by means of an extrajudicial decree.

§4 The pronouncements of this Supreme Tribunal, rendered within the limits of its proper competence, do not need to be submitted for the approval of the Supreme Pontiff.

Art. 10

§1 Whenever the Ordinary or Hierarch receives a report of a more grave delict, which has at least the semblance of truth, and after having completed the preliminary investigation according to the norm of can. 1717 *CIC* and can. 1468 *CCEO*, he is to communicate the matter to the Congregation for the Doctrine of the Faith which, unless it calls the case to itself due to particular circumstances, will direct the Ordinary or Hierarch how to proceed further.

§2 The Ordinary or Hierarch may impose, from the beginning of the preliminary investigation, those measures which are established in can. 1722 *CIC* or in can. 1473 *CCEO*.

§3 If a case is referred directly to the Congregation without a preliminary investigation having been undertaken, the initial steps of the process, which fall by common law to the Ordinary or Hierarch, may be carried out by the Congregation itself, which will provide for those matters either directly or through its Delegate.

Art. 11

With full respect for the right of defense, the Congregation for the Doctrine of the Faith may sanate the acts in cases involving delicts reserved to itself, if merely procedural laws have been violated.

Title Two: Concerning the Judicial Process

Art. 12

§1 The Members of the Congregation for the Doctrine of the Faith are *ipso iure* the judges of this Supreme Tribunal.

§2 The Prefect of the Congregation presides as first among equals over the Tribunal, and, if the office of the Prefect is vacant or if the Prefect himself is impeded, the Secretary of the Congregation carries out his duties.

§3 It is likewise the responsibility of the Prefect of the Congregation to appoint other judges.

Art. 13

In all Tribunals dealing with the cases which are mentioned in these Norms, the following are able to validly fulfill the functions of:

1° Judge and Promoter of Justice, only priests possessing a doctoral degree or at least a license in canon law, outstanding in good morals, prudence, and expertise in the law;

2° Notary and Chancellor, only priests with a blameless reputation and above all suspicion;

3° Advocate and Procurator, members of the faithful possessing a doctoral degree or at least a license in canon law, who are to be admitted by the presiding judge of the college.

Art. 14

In individual cases, the Congregation for the Doctrine of the Faith is able to grant dispensations from the requirement of priesthood.

Art. 15

The presiding judge of the tribunal, having heard the Promoter of Justice, enjoys the same power mentioned in art. 10 §2.

Art. 16

§1 Once an instance before another Tribunal has been finished in any manner, all of the acts of the case are to be transmitted *ex officio* to the Congregation for the Doctrine of the Faith as soon as possible.

§2 The accused and the Promoter of Justice of the Supreme Tribunal of the Congregation for the Doctrine of the Faith may lodge an appeal to the Tribunal within the peremptory time limit of sixty useful days from the publication of the sentence of first instance.

§3 The appeal must be proposed before the Supreme Tribunal of the Congregation which, except in the case of conferral of this responsibility to another Tribunal, judges in the second instance cases having been determined in the first instance by other Tribunals, or by the Supreme Apostolic Tribunal itself in another collegial composition.

§4 No appeal is admitted before the Supreme Tribunal of the Congregation against a sentence if it relates solely to other delicts mentioned in art. 9 §2.

Art. 17

If, in the appellate stage, the Promoter of Justice brings forth a specifically different accusation, this Supreme Tribunal may admit and judge it, as if it were in the first instance.

Art. 18

A *res iudicata* occurs:

1° if a sentence has been rendered in second instance;

2° if an appeal was not proposed within the time limit mentioned in art. 16 §2;

3° if, in the appellate grade, the instance is abated or is renounced.

Title Three: Concerning the Extrajudicial Process

Art. 19

§1 Whenever the Congregation for the Doctrine of the Faith has decided that an extrajudicial process should be initiated, can. 1720 *CIC* or can. 1486 *CCEO* is to be applied.

§2 With the prior mandate of the Congregation for the Doctrine of the Faith, perpetual expiatory penalties may be imposed.

Art. 20

§1 The extrajudicial process may be carried out by the Congregation for the Doctrine of the Faith or by an Ordinary or Hierarch or by their Delegate.

§2 The function of Delegate can be discharged only by priests possessing a doctoral degree or at least a license in canon law, outstanding in good morals, prudence, and expertise in the law.

§3 According to the norm of can. 1720 *CIC*, the requirements mentioned in can. 1424 *CIC* apply to the function of the Assessor in this process.

§4 The one who conducts the investigation cannot undertake the functions mentioned in §§2 and 3.

§5 According to the norm of can. 1486 *CCEO*, only priests possessing a doctoral degree or at least a license in canon law, outstanding in good morals, prudence, and expertise in the law are able to carry out the function of Promoter of Justice.

§6 Only priests with a blameless reputation and above all suspicion are able to carry out the function of Notary.

§7 The defendant must always utilize an Advocate or Procurator, who must be a member of the faithful with a doctoral degree or at least a license in canon law, admitted by the Congregation for the Doctrine of the Faith or by the Ordinary or the Hierarch or by their Delegate. Should the defendant not provide one for himself, the competent authority shall name one who will remain in office only until such time as the defendant appoints one himself.

Art. 21

The Congregation for the Doctrine of the Faith may grant dispensations from the requirements of priesthood and of academic degrees mentioned in art. 20.

Art. 22

With the extrajudicial process having been completed in any manner, all of the acts of the case are to be transmitted *ex officio* to the Congregation for the Doctrine of the Faith as soon as possible.

Art. 23

§1 In accord with the norm of can. 1734 *CIC*, the Promoter of Justice of the Congregation for the Doctrine of the Faith and the defendant have the right to petition in writing for the revocation or correction of the decree issued by the Ordinary or by his Delegate in accordance with can. 1720, 3° *CIC*.

§2 Only afterwards may the Promoter of Justice of the Congregation for the Doctrine of the Faith and the defendant, having observed the provisions of can. 1735 *CIC*, make hierarchical recourse to the *Congresso* of the same Dicastery according to the norm of can. 1737 *CIC*.

§3 Against the decree issued by the Hierarch or by his Delegate *ex* can. 1486, §1, 3° *CCEO*, the Promoter of Justice of the Congregation for the Doctrine of the Faith and the defendant may present hierarchical recourse to the *Congresso* of the same Dicastery, in accord with can. 1487 *CCEO*.

§4 No recourse is admitted before the *Congresso* of the Congregation for the Doctrine of the Faith against a decree if it pertains solely to the other delicts mentioned in art. 9 §2.

Art. 24

§1 Against singular administrative acts of the Congregation for the Doctrine of the Faith in cases of reserved delicts, the Promoter of Justice of the Dicastery and the accused have the right to present recourse within the peremptory term of sixty useful days to the same Congregation, which judges the merits and legitimacy of the recourse, excluding any further recourse whatsoever as described in art. 123 of the Apostolic Constitution *Pastor bonus*.

§2 In order to present the recourse referred to in §1, the accused must, on pain of the inadmissibility of the same recourse, always avail himself of the services of an Advocate who should be a member of the faithful, possessing the appropriate mandate and possessing a doctorate or at least a licentiate in canon law.

§3 The recourse mentioned in §1, in order to be admitted, must clearly indicate the *petitum* and contain the reasons *in iure* and *in facto* on which it is based.

Art. 25

An extrajudicial penal decree becomes definitive:

1° where the period of time mentioned in can. 1734 §2 *CIC* or in can. 1737 §2 *CIC* has elapsed without action;

2° where the period of time mentioned in can. 1487 §1 *CCEO* has elapsed without action;

3° where the period of time mentioned in art. 24 §1 of the present Norms has elapsed without action;

4° when it has been issued by the Congregation for the Doctrine of the Faith pursuant to art. 24 §1 of these present Norms.

Title Four: Final Dispositions

Art. 26

It is the right of the Congregation for the Doctrine of the Faith, in whatever stage and grade of the unfolding of the proceedings, to present directly the most grave cases mentioned above in artt. 2-6 to the decision of the Supreme Pontiff with regard to dismissal or deposition from the clerical state, together with dispensation from the law of celibacy, when it is manifestly evident that the delict has been committed, after having given the guilty party the possibility of defending himself.

Art. 27

It is the right of the accused, in whatever moment, to request from the Supreme Pontiff, through the Congregation for the Doctrine of the Faith, a dispensation from all the obligations deriving from sacred ordination, including celibacy, and, should it be the case, from religious profession.

Art. 28

§1 With the exception of allegations, processes, and decisions concerning the delicts mentioned in art. 6, cases involving delicts regulated by these Norms are subject to the pontifical secret.

§2 Whoever has violated the secret, whether deliberately (*ex dolo*) or through grave negligence, or has caused some harm to the accused or to witnesses or to those involved in the penal case in any manner, at the request of the injured party or even *ex officio,* shall be punished by means of suitable penalties.

Art. 29

In these cases, together with the prescripts of these Norms, the canons concerning delicts and penalties as well as the canons concerning the penal process of each Code also must be applied.

Address of His Holiness Pope Francis to the Officials of the Tribunal of the Roman Rota for the Inauguration of the Judicial Year

27 January 2022

Address of the Holy Father

Your Excellency,

Dear Prelate Auditors,

I address my cordial greeting to each one of us, starting from the Dean, Msgr. Alejandro Arellano Cedillo, whom I thank for his words. And thank you for the last two things you asked the Pope for: comfort and blessing. I like this. It is a pastoral request. Thank you.

I greet the officials, the attorneys and the other collaborators of the Apostolic Tribunal of the Roman Rota. I extend my best wishes for the judicial year that we inaugurate today.

The synodal path we are undertaking also challenges this meeting of ours, because it also involves the judicial sphere and your mission at the service of families, especially those who are wounded, those in need of the balm of mercy.[1] In this year dedicated to the family as an expression of the joy of love, today we have the opportunity to reflect on synodality in matrimonial nullity proceedings. Although synodal work is not strictly procedural in nature, it should be placed in dialogue with judicial activity, in order to encourage a more general rethinking of the importance of the experience of the canonical process for the lives of the faithful who have experienced a marriage breakdown and, at the same time, for the harmony of relationships within the ecclesial community. Let us then ask ourselves in what sense the administration of justice needs a synodal spirit.

First and foremost, synodality implies *walking together*. Overcoming a distorted view of marriage cases, as if they were concerned with merely subjective interests, it must be rediscovered that all the participants in the case are required to contribute towards the same objective, that of shining a light on the truth of a real union between a man and a woman, arriving at the conclusion regarding the existence or otherwise of a true marriage between them. This view of walking together towards a common goal is not new in the ecclesial understanding of these cases. In this regard, the Venerable Pius XII's address to the Roman Rota, is well-

1 Bull Misericordiae Vultus 5: *AAS* 107 [2015], 402.

known; in it, he refers to – I quote – "the unity of purpose, which must give special form to the work and collaboration of all those who participate in the treatment of marriage cases in ecclesiastical tribunals of every level and type, and must inspire and join them in the same unity of purpose and action,"[2] end quote. From this perspective, he outlined the task of every participant in the case with regard to the search for truth, while maintaining the fidelity of each to their role. This truth, if it is truly loved, becomes liberating.[3]

Already in the pre-judicial phase, when the faithful find themselves in difficulty and look for pastoral help, there can be no lack of effort to discover the truth on the union, an indispensable prerequisite for the healing of wounds. In this context, one can understand the importance of commitment to promoting forgiveness and reconciliation between spouses, and also, eventually, to confirming the nullity of marriage where this is possible and prudent. In this way it may also be understood that the declaration of nullity must not be presented as if it were the sole objective to be reached when faced with a marriage crisis, or as if it constituted a right regardless of the facts. When presenting the possibility of nullity, it is necessary to make the faithful reflect on the reasons that lead them to ask for a declaration of nullity of their matrimonial consent, thus encouraging an attitude of acceptance of the final judgement, even if it does not correspond to their own convictions. Only in this way can nullity proceedings be an expression of effective pastoral accompaniment of the faithful in their matrimonial crises, which means listening to the Holy Spirit who speaks in the concrete history of individuals. Two or three years ago we spoke of the matrimonial catechumenate. Before, the first years ... [sentence unfinished].

The same objective of the shared pursuit of the truth must characterize every phase of the judicial process. It is true that in a trial there is sometimes a dialectic between contrasting theses; however, the adversarial process between the parties should always take place in sincere adherence to what appears to be true for each party, without closing in on one's own vision, but being open to the contribution of the other participants in the process. The willingness to offer one's own subjective version of the facts becomes fruitful in the context of adequate communication with others, which can also reach self-criticism. Therefore, any deliberate alteration or manipulation of the facts in order to achieve a pragmatically desired result is inadmissible. Here I pause and apologize for stating a very great danger. When one does not overcome this, even lawyers can do terrible damage. A month ago a bishop came to complain because he had a

---

2 Address to the Roman Rota, 2 October 1944: *AAS* 36 [1944], 281.

3 Cfr Gv 8:32.

problem with a priest. A serious problem. It wasn't marriage that was the problem; [it was] a serious discipline problem that deserved to go to trial. The bishop's lawyer, whom the bishop ... not the lawyer, sorry. The judge of the national court—I am not talking about that country or that country; a country—called the bishop and said, "I have received this. I will do what you tell me. If you tell me to condemn him, I will condemn him; if you tell me to absolve him, I will absolve him." This can happen, it can come to this if there is not this unity in the processes even with conflicting sentences; go ahead together, for the good of the Church, the good of the people! It is a matter of negotiation. Excuse me, but this anecdote enlightened me a lot.

Going together towards the judgement applies to the parties and to their patrons, to the witnesses who are called upon to testify in accordance with the truth, for the experts who must place their knowledge at the service of the trial, and in a special way for the judges. Indeed, the administration of justice in the Church is a manifestation of the care of souls, which requires pastoral solicitude in order to be servants of salvific truth and mercy. This *ministerium veritatis* takes on a particular significance in bishops, when they judge in the first person, especially in shorter trials, and when they exercise their responsibility towards their own courts, thus also showing their paternal solicitude towards the faithful. And I return to something that I have always said from the first moment: the original judge is the bishop. The dean greeted me by [saying] with "the Pope, Supreme Judge *pro toto orbe catholico* . . ." of all the Catholic world. But this is because I am bishop of Rome, and Rome presides over everything; not because I have another title. Thank you for that. But, if the Pope has that power is it because he is bishop of the diocese whose bishop the Lord has willed to be the Pope. The true and first is the bishop, not the judicial vicar, no. The bishop.

Synodality in trials implies a *constant exercise of listening*. Here, too, it is necessary to learn to *listen*, which is not simply *hearing*. Listening is not just hearing. That is, it is necessary to understand the vision and reasons of the other, almost to identify with the other. As in other areas of pastoral care, a culture of listening, which is a prerequisite for a culture of encounter, must also be fostered in judicial activity. This is why standard answers to the concrete problems of individual persons are harmful. Each person, with his or her experience, often marked by pain, constitutes for the ecclesiastical judge the real "existential periphery" from which every judicial pastoral action must set out.

The trial also requires careful listening to what is argued and demonstrated by the parties. Of particular importance is the preliminary investigation aimed at establishing the facts, which requires those who lead it to know how to combine the right professionalism with closeness and listening. Does this take time? Yes, it takes time. Does it require patience? Yes, it requires patience. Does it require pastoral paternity? Yes, it requires pastoral paternity. Judges must be listeners *par excellence* of everything that has emerged in the trial for and against the declaration of nullity. They are bound to do so by virtue of a duty of justice, animated and sustained by pastoral charity. In fact, "mercy is the fullness of justice and the most radiant manifestation of God's truth" (Post-Synodal Apostolic Exhortation *Amoris Laetitia*, 311). Moreover, when - as is usually the case - there is a panel of judges, each judge must be open to the reasons presented by the other members in order to arrive at a considered judgement. In this sense, in your action as ministers of the court, you must never lack a pastoral heart, a spirit of charity and understanding towards persons who suffer from the failure of their married life. To acquire such a style, it is necessary to avoid the dead end of legalism—which is a kind of legal Pelagianism, isn't it? It is not Catholic. Juridicism is not Catholic—that is, a self-referential view of the law. Law and judgement are always at the service of truth, justice and the evangelical virtue of charity.

Another aspect of synodal processes is discernment, because the synod is not just asking for opinions, it is not an enquiry—what do you say? and you, and you? No: what one says is part of discernment, the ability to discern. And discernment is not easy. It is a discernment based on walking together and listening, and which allows one to read the real matrimonial situation in the light of the Word of God and the Magisterium of the Church. The judges' decision thus appears as a way of entering into the reality of a vital event, in order to discover in it the existence or otherwise of that irrevocable event which is the valid consent on which marriage is founded. Only in this way can the laws relating to individual forms of matrimonial nullity be fruitfully applied, inasmuch as they are expressions of the doctrine and discipline of the Church on marriage. This is where the prudence of law operates, in its classic sense of *recta ratio agibilium*, that is, the virtue that judges according to reason, that is, with rectitude in the practical sphere. Returning to that example: "What do you want? Do I condemn him or free him?"

The outcome of this journey is the *judgement*, the fruit of careful discernment that leads to an authoritative word of truth about personal experience, thus highlighting the paths that can be opened up from there. The judgement must therefore be comprehensible to the persons involved: only in this way will it become a moment of special significance in their human and Christian journey.

Dear prelate auditors, these considerations, which I would like to bring to your attention, show how the dimension of synodality makes it possible to highlight the essential characteristics of the process. I encourage you, therefore, to continue with fidelity and renewed industriousness your ecclesial ministry at the service of justice, inseparable from truth and, ultimately, from the *salus animarum.* This work manifests the merciful face of the Church: a maternal face that bends down over every member of the faithful to help them to make the truth about themselves, lifting them up from their defeats and labors and inviting them to live to the full the beauty of the Gospel.

I reiterate my esteem and gratitude to each one of you. I ask the Holy Spirit to accompany your activity always and I bless you from my heart. And do not forget to pray. May prayer always accompany you. "I am busy, I have so many things to do . . . ." The first thing you must do is pray. Pray that the Lord may be close to you. And also to know the heart of the Lord: we know him in prayer. And judges should pray, and they must pray twice or three times as much. Please also, don't forget to pray for me. You understand. Thank you.

POPE FRANCIS

Implementing the Modification of Multiple Canons from the Latin and Eastern Codes

Unofficial English Translation

Apostolic Letter Issued "Motu Proprio"
of the Supreme Pontiff Francis

Competentias Quasdam Decernere

Introducing Changes to Some Norms of the Code of Canon Law
and the Code of Canons of the Eastern Churches

The assignment of certain areas of competence with regard to the provisions of the Codes intended to safeguard unity of discipline in the universal Church, and executive power in the local Churches and ecclesial institutions, corresponds to the dynamic of ecclesiastical communion and enhances proximity. A healthy decentralization can only foster that dynamic, without prejudice to its hierarchical dimension.

Therefore, with due regard for the ecclesial culture and juridical mentality proper to each code, I have considered it fitting to introduce changes to the current regulations in certain specific areas, by assigning their various areas of competence. They are meant, above all, to foster the sense of collegiality and pastoral responsibility of diocesan/eparchial bishops assembled in episcopal conferences, or in accordance with eastern hierarchical structures, and major superiors, but also to respect the principles of reasonableness, effectiveness and efficiency.

These changes reflect more clearly the Church's shared and pluralistic universality, which embraces differences without leveling them, guaranteeing, with respect to her unity, the ministry of the Bishop of Rome. At the same time, they will encourage a more rapid and effective pastoral governance on the part of local authority, not least by facilitating its proximity to individuals and situations that demand it.

Wherefore, I now decree the following:

Art. 1

Canon 237 §2 CIC, on the erection of an interdiocesan seminary and its statutes, replaces the term "approval" with the term "confirmation," and now reads:

§2. An interdiocesan seminary is not to be erected unless the conference of bishops, if the seminary is for its entire territory, or the bishops involved have obtained the prior confirmation of the Apostolic See for both the erection of the seminary and its statutes.

Art. 2

Canon 242 §1 CIC concerning the program of priestly formation established by the episcopal conference replaces the term "approved" with the term "confirmed," and now reads:

§1. Each nation is to have a program of priestly formation which is to be established by the conference of bishops, attentive to the norms issued by the supreme authority of the Church, and which is to be confirmed by the Holy See. This program is to be adapted to new circumstances, also with the confirmation of the Holy See, and is to define the main principles of the instruction to be given in the seminary and general norms adapted to the pastoral needs of each region or province.

Art. 3

Canon 265 CIC, on incardination, adds to the structures that can incardinate clerics public clerical associations which have received that faculty from the Holy See, thereby harmonizing this canon with canon 357 §1 CCEO. The text of the canon now reads:

Every cleric must be incardinated either in a particular church or personal prelature, or in an institute of consecrated life or society endowed with this faculty, or also in a public clerical association that has obtained that faculty from the Apostolic See, in such a way that unattached or transient clerics are not allowed at all.

Art. 4

Canon 604 CIC, on the order of virgins and their right to associate, includes a new paragraph formulated as follows:

§3. The diocesan bishop is competent for the recognition and erection of such associations at the diocesan level, within his territory; the conference of bishops is competent at the national level, within its own territory.

Art. 5

Canons 686 §1 CIC and 489 §2 CCEO, on the grant of an indult of exclaustration, for a grave cause, to a member professed by perpetual vows, extend the time limit for five years, after which, competence for an extension or grant is reserved to the Holy See or to the diocesan bishop. The text now reads:

CIC – can. 686 §1: With the consent of the council, the supreme moderator for a grave cause can grant an indult of exclaustration to a member professed by perpetual vows, but not for more than five years, and if it concerns a cleric, with the prior consent of the ordinary of the place in which he must reside. To extend an indult or to grant it for more than five years is reserved to the Holy See, or to the diocesan bishop if it concerns institutes of diocesan right.

CCEO – can. 489 § 2: The eparchial bishop can grant this indult only for up to five years.

Art. 6

Canon 688 §2 CIC and canons 496 §§1-2 and 546 §2 CCEO, on individuals temporarily professed who ask, for a grave cause, to leave the institute, assign competence for the relevant indult to the supreme moderator, with the consent of the council. For the Latin Code, this applies to both institutes of pontifical right and institutes of diocesan right, as well as autonomous monasteries; for the Eastern Code, it applies to a monastery sui iuris or to an order or congregation.

Consequently, canon 496 §2 CCEO is eliminated; the other canons now read:

CIC – can. 688 §2: During the time of temporary profession, a person who asks to leave the institute for a grave cause can obtain an indult of departure from the supreme moderator with the consent of his or her council; in the case of an autonomous monastery, mentioned in can. 615, however, the bishop of the house of assignment must confirm the indult for it to be valid.

CCEO – can. 496: One who during temporary profession wishes for a grave cause to leave the monastery and return to secular life is to present a petition to his or her superior of the monastery *sui iuris*. The superior, with the consent of his or her council, grants the indult, unless particular law reserves this to the patriarch for monasteries located within the territorial boundaries of the patriarchal Church.

CCEO – can. 546 §2: One who, while still in temporary vows, requests for a grave cause to leave the order or congregation, can obtain from the superior general with the consent of his or her council the indult to leave the order definitively and return to secular life, with the effects mentioned in can. 493.

Art. 7

Canons 699 §2 and 700 CIC and canons 499, 501 §2 and 552 §1 CCEO are modified, so that that the decree of dismissal from an institute, for a grave cause, of a temporarily or perpetually professed member takes effect from the time that the decree, issued by the supreme moderator with the consent of his or her council, is communicated to that member, who retains the right to appeal. The texts of the respective canons are thus modified and reformulated as follows:

CIC – can. 699 §2: In the autonomous monasteries mentioned in can. 615, it belongs to the major superior, with the consent of his or her council, to decide on dismissal.

CIC – can. 700: A decree of dismissal issued in the case of a professed member takes effect from the time that it is communicated to the member concerned. To be valid, however, the decree must indicate the right that the dismissed possesses to make recourse to the competent authority within ten days from receiving notification. The recourse has suspensive effect.

CCEO – can. 499: A member can be dismissed during temporary profession by the superior of the monastery *sui iuris* with the consent of his or her council according to can. 552 §§2 and 3, but, for validity, the dismissal must be confirmed by the patriarch if particular law so establishes for monasteries situated with the territorial boundaries of the patriarchal Church.

CCEO – can. 501 §2: However, the member can, within fifteen days, either make recourse with suspensive effect against the decree of dismissal or request that the case be handled judicially.

CCEO – can. 552 §1: A member in temporary vows can be dismissed by the superior general with the consent of his or her council.

Art. 8

Canon 775 §2 CIC, on the publication of catechisms by an episcopal conference for its own territory, replaces the term "approval" with the term "confirmation", and now reads:

§2: If it seems useful, it is for the conference of bishops to take care that catechisms are issued for its territory, with the previous confirmation of the Apostolic See.

Art. 9

Canon 1308 CIC and canon 1052 CCEO, on reducing the obligations of Masses, modify competence, and now read:

CIC – can. 1308 §1: A reduction of the obligations of Masses, to be made only for a just and necessary cause, is reserved to the diocesan bishop and to the supreme moderator of a clerical institute of consecrated life or a society of apostolic life.

§2: With regard to Masses independently founded in legacies, the diocesan bishop has the power, because of diminished revenues and for as long as the cause exists, to reduce the obligations to the level of offering legitimately established in the diocese, provided that there is no one obliged to increase the offering who can effectively be made to do so.

§3: The diocesan bishop also has the power to reduce the obligations or legacies of Masses binding an ecclesiastical institute if the revenue has become insufficient to pursue appropriately the proper purpose of the institute.

§4: The supreme moderator of a clerical institute of consecrated life or a society of apostolic life possesses the same powers mentioned in §§2 and 3.

CCEO – can. 1052 §1: A reduction of the obligations of celebrating the Divine Liturgy is reserved to the eparchial bishop and to the major superior of religious institutes or societies of common life according to the manner of religious that are clerical.

§2: An eparchial bishop has the power, because of a diminution of revenues and while this lasts, to reduce the number of the celebrations of the Divine Liturgy to the level of the offerings legitimately in force in the eparchy, provided there is no one who is bound by obligation and can effectively be forced to increase the offering.

§3: An eparchial bishop also has the power to reduce the obligations of celebrating the Divine Liturgy which burden ecclesiastical institutes, if the revenues have become insufficient to pursue those purposes which, at the time of the acceptance of the same obligations, could have been obtained.

§4: Superiors general of clerical religious institutes or societies of common life according to the manner of religious also have the powers mentioned in §§2 and 3.

§5: An eparchial bishop can delegate the powers mentioned in §§2 and 3 only to a coadjutor bishop, auxiliary bishop, protosyncellus or syncellus, excluding any subdelegation.

Art. 10

Canon 1310 CIC and canon 1054 CCEO on the obligations connected to pious causes and pious foundations modify competence, and now read:

CIC – can. 1310 §1: The ordinary, only for a just and necessary cause, can reduce, moderate or commute the wills of the faithful for pious causes, after having heard those concerned and his own finance council and with the intention of the founder preserved as much as possible.

§2: In other cases, recourse is to be made to the Apostolic See.

CCEO – can. 1054 §1: The hierarch, only for a just and necessary cause, can reduce, moderate or commute the wills of the Christian faithful who give or leave their goods for pious causes, after having heard those concerned and the competent council and having kept in the best way possible the will of the founder.

§2: In other cases regarding this matter, the Apostolic See or the patriarch must be approached; the latter is to act with the consent of the permanent synod.

All that I have determined in this Apostolic Letter issued "Motu Proprio", I order to have full and stable effect, anything to the contrary notwithstanding, even if worthy of particular mention, and I decree that it be promulgated by publication in "*L'Osservatore Romano,*" to take effect on 15 February 2022, and subsequently be published in the official commentary *Acta Apostolicae Sedis.*

Given in Rome, at Saint Peter's, on 11 February, the Memorial of Our Lady of Lourdes, in the year 2022, the ninth of my Pontificate.

FRANCIS

THE SUPREME PONTIFF FRANCIS

APOSTOLIC LETTER
ISSUED MOTU PROPRIO

REVISED BOOK VI

BY WHICH CAN. 695 §1 OF THE CODE OF CANON LAW IS MODIFIED

The revised Book VI of the Code of Canon Law, *On Penal Sanctions in the Church*, Apostolic Constitution *Pascite gregem Dei*, was promulgated on June 1, 2021. In this book the account of certain offenses was changed, some new offenses were introduced, and the numerical order of the canons has also been modified. In order that all these things may be in harmony with the canons of the other books of the Code, adaptation is required.

Having heard these things before the Pontifical Council for Legislative Texts and the Congregation for Institutes of Consecrated Life and Societies of Apostolic Life, we have decided that hereafter can. 695 §1 is to be drafted:

> *A member must be released for the delicts mentioned in cann. 1395, 1397 and 1398, unless in the delicts mentioned in cann. 1395 §§2-3 and 1398 §1, the major superior decides that dismissal is not completely necessary at all and that correction of the member, restitution of justice, and reparation of scandal can be resolved sufficiently in another way.*

Whatever decrees were given by these Apostolic Letters Motu Proprio, we hold firm and ratified, to the contrary, whatsoever, even worthy of special mention, notwithstanding, bidding that they be promulgated by publication in the daily acts of *L'Osservatore Romano* and shall come into force o the same day and then to be published in the official commentary *Acta Apostolica Sedis*.

Given in Rome, at Saint Peter's, on the twenty-sixth of April, in the year 2022, the tenth of Our Pontificate

POPE FRANCIS

Rescriptum Ex Audientia Ss.mi:

Rescript of the Holy Father Francis regarding the Derogation from Can. 588 §2 *CIC*

18 May 2022

Archbishop Secretary has granted the Congregation for Institutes of Consecrated Life and Societies of Apostolic Life the faculty to authorize, at the discretion and in individual cases, to non-clerical associates the conferment of the office of major superior in clerical religious institutes of pontifical right and in clerical societies of apostolic life of pontifical right of the Latin Church and dependent on it, notwithstanding can. 588 §2 *CIC* and the proper law of the institute of consecrated life or of the society of apostolic life, without prejudice to can. 134 §1.

1. A non-cleric companion of an institute of consecrated life or a society of clerical apostolic life of pontifical right is appointed local superior by the supreme moderator with the consent of his council.

2. A non-cleric companion of an institute of consecrated life or of a clerical society of apostolic life of pontifical right is appointed major superior, after having obtained a written license from the Congregation for Institutes of Consecrated Life and Societies of Apostolic Life at the request of the supreme moderator with the consent of the council.

3. A non-cleric fellow member of an institute of consecrated life or of a society of clerical apostolic life of pontifical right elected supreme moderator or major superior, according to the modalities provided for by proper law, requires confirmation—by written license—of the Congregation for Institutes of Consecrated Life and Societies of Apostolic Life.

4. In the cases provided for in §§2-3, the Congregation for Institutes of Consecrated Life and Societies of Apostolic Life reserves the right to evaluate the individual case and the reasons given by the supreme moderator or by the general chapter.

The Holy Father also ordered that this Rescript be published in *L'Osservatore Romano*, and subsequently in the official commentary of the *Acta Apostolicae Sedis*, entering into force today.

From the Vatican, 18 May 2022.

João Braz Card. de Aviz
Prefetto

José Rodríguez Carballo, O.F.M.
Arcivescovo Segretario

Rescriptum Ex Audientia Ss.Mi:

Rescritto Del Santo Padre Francesco Circa Le Associazioni Pubbliche Di Fedeli In Itinere

Il Santo Padre Francesco, nell'Udienza concessa il 7 febbraio u.s. ai sottoscritti Cardinale Prefetto e Arcivescovo Segretario del Dicastero per gli Istituti di vita consacrata e le Società di vita apostolica ha approvato in forma specifica il seguente disposto:

"Il Vescovo diocesano prima di erigere – mediante decreto – un'associazione pubblica di fedeli in vista di diventare Istituto di vita consacrata o Società di vita apostolica di diritto diocesano, deve ottenere la licenza scritta del Dicastero per gli Istituti di Vita consacrata e le Società di vita apostolica".

Il Santo Padre ha altresì disposto che il presente Rescritto sia promulgato tramite pubblicazione su *L'Osservatore Romano*, entrando in vigore immediatamente, e quindi pubblicato nel commentario ufficiale degli *Acta Apostolicae Sedis*.

Dal Vaticano, 15 giugno 2022

João Braz Card. de Aviz	José Rodríguez Carballo, O.F.M.
Prefetto	*Arcivescovo Segretario*

****

Unofficial Translation

RESCRIPT OF THE HOLY FATHER FRANCIS ABOUT THE PUBLIC ASSOCIATIONS OF FAITHFUL *IN ITINERE*

The Holy Father Francis, in the audience granted on 7 February this year to the undersigned Cardinal Prefect and Archbishop Secretary of the Dicastery for Institutes of Consecrated Life and Societies of Apostolic Life has specifically approved the following provision:

"Before the diocesan bishop erects—by decree—a public association of the faithful with a view to becoming an institute of consecrated life or a society of apostolic life of diocesan right, he must obtain the written license of the Dicastery for Institutes of Consecrated Life and Societies of Apostolic Life."

The Holy Father also ordered that this Rescript be promulgated through publication in *L'Osservatore Romano*, entering into force immediately, and then published in the official commentary of the *Acta Apostolicae Sedis*.

From the Vatican, 15 June 2022

ADVISORY OPINIONS

Introductory Note

The following opinions were assembled by the editors for the advisory opinions section of this publication from among the opinions submitted to the Society for publication. The editors are members of the Publications Advisory Board. The opinions carry only the weight of the person(s) named at the end of each opinion. They do not represent the opinion of the diocese or institution to which the author is affiliated, nor that of the Canon Law Society of America. Advisory opinions are not authentic interpretations of the law but reflect the scholarly and practical insights of the contributors.

The opinions are arranged according to the canons of the *Code of Canon Law,* the *Code of Canons of the Eastern Churches*, and occasionally other documents of canonical import. The original questions or situations have been abbreviated or summarized, and the opinions lightly edited to protect the anonymity of the inquirer and to conform to the style of Canon Law Society of America publications.

The Publications Advisory Board expresses gratitude to the canonists who participated in this year's publication. The continued success of this annual project is a result of their willingness to share their time and talent in service to this important work.

The Canon Law Society of America is interested in receiving opinions that members have formulated in response to specific inquiries and inquiries in need of responses. It also welcomes the participation of members who wish to be involved in this annual project by offering to render opinions to inquiries received by the Board of Governors or the Executive Coordinator.

Inquiries or contributions may be directed by mail or email to:

Executive Coordinator
Canon Law Society of America
415 Michigan Avenue NE, Suite 101
Washington, DC 20017-4502

ExecutiveCoordinator@clsa.org

CANON 128

RESPONSIBILITY AND LIABILITY FOR REPAIR OF HARM TO ABUSE VICTIMS

The Royal Commission into Abuse in Care in New Zealand[1] *and the Australian Royal Commission into Institutional Responses to Child Sexual Abuse*[2] *have both had serious questions about the relationship of diocesan bishops and religious institutes. Commissioners in both these commissions struggled to understand the complex governance relationships in the Catholic Church.*

OPINION

Priests act in the name of the Church[3] and religious are in a permanent state recognised by the Church.[4] However, since Vatican II there have been significant changes in law concerning entrusted and proper works of religious, and what oversight and responsibility has meant in practice.[5] Religious superiors have often asserted their independence from diocesan bishops, contrary to canon law. Many religious superiors are still not observing their obligation to notify local Ordinaries of reports of abuse.

In 2019, Pope Francis in *Vos estis lux mundi*[6] introduced mandatory reporting of sexual abuse by clerics and religious within the Church. Article 3 stated:

> §1. Except as provided for by canons 1548 §2 *CIC* and 1229 §2 *CCEO*, whenever a cleric or a member of an Institute of Consecrated Life or of a Society of Apostolic Life has notice of, or well-founded motives to believe that, one of the facts referred to in article 1 has been committed, that person is obliged to report promptly the fact to the local Ordinary where the events are said to have occurred or to another Ordinary among those referred to in canons 134 *CIC* and 984 *CCEO*, except for what is established by §3 of the present article.

---

1 See https://www.abuseincare.org.nz/.

2 See https://www.childabuseroyalcommission.gov.au/.

3 See *Catechism of the Catholic Church* (*CCC*) 1552.

4 See *CCC* 915.

5 See Benjamin Earl OP, "Opera Propria: property or patrimony? Consequences for mutual relations between Bishops and Religious," *The Canon Law Society of Great Britain and Ireland Newsletter*, November 2021, no. 200, 33-53.

6 See Francis, motu proprio, *Vos estis lux mundi,* 7 May 2019 (*VELM*), http://w2.vatican.va/content/francesco/en/motu_proprio/documents/papa-francesco-motu-proprio-20190507vos-estis-lux-mundi.html.

§2. Any person can submit a report concerning the conduct referred to in article 1, using the methods referred to in the preceding article, or by any other appropriate means.

§3. When the report concerns one of the persons indicated in article 6, it is to be addressed to the Authority identified based upon articles 8 and 9. The report can always be sent to the Holy See directly or through the Pontifical Representative.

§4. The report shall include as many particulars as possible, such as indications of time and place of the facts, of the persons involved or informed, as well as any other circumstance that may be useful in order to ensure an accurate assessment of the facts.

§5. Information can also be acquired *ex officio*.[7]

Some diocesan bishops believed canon 384 justified them giving priests leniency in dealing with complaints about their abuse or misconduct. While bishops have a responsibility to defend and care for their priests, it is vital that they do not take one canon alone without taking into account the whole Code of Canon Law and all other canonical documents.

Bishops also have a responsibility to care for all the faithful in their dioceses. Diocesan bishops are responsible for caring for victims.

1. Bishops and Religious

The authority of diocesan bishops to members of religious institutes is summarised by Kozlowski:

> [A]ll members are subject to the diocesan bishop. . . . The extent of the authority that a diocesan bishop exercises over a member of a religious institute, then, is largely dependent on the member's engagement in the external apostolate in conjunction with the nature of the apostolic work (i.e., is the work proper to the institute or is it entrusted to the institute or one of its members by the diocesan bishop?). At the same time, the member must still obey the legitimate commands of his/her religious superiors (c. 601) and remain faithful to the discipline of the institute (c. 678 §2). Also, this same superior has authority over a religious' exercise of an external apostolate. The extent of the religious superior's authority is also affected by the nature of the work (i.e., proper or entrusted). In short, a religious who exercises an external apostolate is

7 *VELM* art. 3.

> subject to a dual authority structure which consists of the diocesan bishop and religious superior.[8]

The most common apostolate that religious institutes are involved with are schools. The power of the bishop in relation to schools is outlined by Richard Hill:

> According to the 1983 code, whether the school is a proper or entrusted work: "The bishop has the right to establish general policies for all Catholic schools (c. 806 §1), to supervise religious formation and education imparted in schools (c. 804 §1), to approve the appointment of those who are to teach religion and to require their removal if he judges this necessary for reasons of religion or morals (c. 805)." If the school is a proper work of the institute, "the right of the religious to direct or manage these schools remains intact (C 806, §1)."[9]

On the relationship between canons 683 §1 and 806 §1, Cito states that the bishop's vigilance function "encompasses everything that could reasonably cause harm to the Catholic character of the educational institution."[10] The local Ordinary, including the diocesan bishop, can remove the faculties of any cleric or, if there is an investigation of an alleged crime,[11] the cleric can be prohibited from the exercise of sacred ministry.[12]

When an individual religious is causing grave scandal, canon 679 provides for a diocesan bishop to expel him or her from the diocese. The reason could be the religious is having an affair with someone or is behaving in another gravely inappropriate manner.

2. Terminating an Apostolate of Religious Institutes

There is no canonical process to terminate an apostolate of a religious institute.[13] However, if religious violate universal or particular law in an apostolate, they can be removed.[14] The bishop grants faculties for a religious to

---

8 Matthew Kozlowski, *A Canonical Analysis of the Authority Exercised by the Diocesan Bishop and the Religious Superior Over the Religious Pastor qua Pastor*, CUA Doctoral dissertation (2021) 4-5.

9 Richard Hill, "The Apostolate of Institutes," in *A Handbook on Canons 573-746,* ed. Jordan Hite et al. (Collegeville, MN: Liturgical Press, 1985) 217.

10 David Cito, in Angel Marzoa, Jorge Miras and Rafael Rodrigues-Ocana, *Exegetical Commentary on the Code of Canon Law*, Vol. 3/1:239 (*Exegetical Commentary*).

11 A crime is a grave or mortal sin classified as a delict in canon law.

12 See c. 1772.

13 See Jordan Hite, TOR, "Mutual Rights and Obligations of Bishops and Major Superiors regarding Public Ministry," *Bulletin on Issues of Religious Law* 14 (Spring 1997) 4.

14 See c. 678 §1.

function publicly in the Church.[15] He can remove those faculties or prohibit the exercise of public ministry.[16]

3. Rights and Obligations of Clerical and Religious Abusers

What is just for abusers is not simple in practice. Abusers have the right to sufficient income for their support if they have not been dismissed from the clerical state or a religious institute.[17] However, if they have been dismissed from the clerical state or their religious institute, any support they receive is given out of charity.

Justice for victims is related to justice for abusers. Morally, abusers should not be getting more income/housing/etc. than their victims and this is quite possible for example if clergy are receiving a stipend and superannuation. If the abuser has assets, the abuser must be forced to compensate their victim by the Ordinary or tribunal.[18]

Natural law and canon law recognise this obligation enshrined in canon 128. The Church, because of its mission, must place particular emphasis on the obligation to repair moral and spiritual harm.[19] This harm to victims must be repaired. Cases vary enormously and the impact of the abuse also varies greatly. This needs to be recognised in each case.

Sometimes abusers receive a punishment of a life of prayer and penance from the Congregation for the Doctrine of the Faith. What this means must be defined in detail by the Conference of Bishops for their territory, so that justice is real, and the punishment does not become a farse.

Lawyers can argue that dioceses and religious institutes are not legally liable for crimes of their clergy, religious and lay employees. There is no doubt however that there is a moral responsibility and liability.

4. Obligations of Dioceses to Victims

The Congregation for the Clergy reminded bishops, in 2009, that ecclesiastical discipline included the obligations of continence[20]:

---

15 See c. 970.

16 See Brendan Daly, "Canon 1336: What processes must the diocesan bishop follow to remove the faculties of a Priest?" in *Roman Replies and CLSA Advisory Opinions 2017* (Washington DC: CLSA, 2017) 87-95.

17 See c. 1350.

18 See c. 128.

19 See G. Michiels OFM, *De delictis et poenis: commentarius libri V Codicis Iuris Canonici,* Editio altera, vol. 1 (Romae: Desclee, 1961) 68-71.

20 Continence means the non-use of the sexual faculties.

> The bishop has, among other things, the duty to remind priests of their obligation to perfect and perpetual continence for the sake of the kingdom of heaven, an obligation freely and willingly assumed by them at the moment of their ordination. Moreover, the bishop must always be attentive that the priest is faithful in carrying out his proper ministerial duties (cf. Canons 384, 392).[21]

However, the priest is not considered an employee or agent of the bishop and is appointed to a parish to do pastoral work such as that outlined in canons 528-529. The Congregation for the Clergy declared:

> The diocesan priest, who is not merely the passive executor of commands received from the bishop, enjoys autonomy in making decisions both in his ministry and in his personal and private life. Thus, he is personally responsible for his personal actions and for those carried out in the scope of his ministry. Consequently, a bishop cannot be held juridically responsible for the acts which a diocesan priest carries out in transgression of the canonical norms, universal or particular. This principle which is not new and has always been part of the patrimony of the church, means, among other things, that the criminal action of a priest, and its penal consequences as well as any eventual payment of damages, is imputable to the priest who has committed the offense and not to the bishop or to the diocese of which the bishop is the legal representative (cf. Canon 393).[22]

However, *Vos estis lux mundi* (*VELM*) has modified this stance by the Congregation for the Clergy in article 5.[23] Pope Francis explained what it meant for diocesan bishops "to be solicitous for all Christ's faithful committed to his care" in *VELM*:

> Article 5 – Care for persons
>
> §1. The ecclesiastical Authorities shall commit themselves to ensuring that those who state that they have been harmed, together with their families, are to be treated with dignity and respect, and, in particular, are to be:
>
> a) welcomed, listened to and supported, including through provision of specific services;
>
> b) offered spiritual assistance;

21 Congregation for the Clergy, Letter, *Origins*, 39 (2008- 2009) 82.

22 Ibid., 83.

23 Cf. footnote 85; *VELM* 5..

c) offered medical assistance, including therapeutic and psychological assistance, as required by the specific case. [24]

It must be acknowledged that in dealing with sexual abuse victims, so many aspects are case specific. General statements do not always serve a just outcome. *Vos estis lux mundi* does not mention financial compensation, but it is a reality for the Church in all western countries. Victims often take a long time to complain. In Australia victims took on average 33 years to seek justice.[25] Religious institutes have a parallel responsibility to victims for those abused by their members.[26]

Dioceses have a responsibility to care for victims of diocesan priests from their diocese.[27] Incardination in a diocese connects the cleric to the diocese which must provide for him in return for his commitment to serve there.[28] If a priest abuser belonged to two dioceses, the dioceses should compensate/help in a proportional manner according to the number of years the priest worked in each diocese. When a diocesan priest offends, he holds the primary responsibility to pay his legal expenses. If he is judged innocent, his diocese has a responsibility to recompense him.

Bishops have more power and responsibility over an entrusted work of a religious institute rather than a proper work. This is because they hold the power to appoint to positions or offices. Consequently, a diocesan bishop appoints a religious priest as a parish priest.[29]

Issues do arise about the bishop's liability as a consequence of his supervisory role over associations of the faithful. "Supervision" [*vigilantia*] in canon 305 is not "governance" or "administration". The diocesan bishop's right of visitation or vigilance over ecclesiastical entities is limited according to the statutes of the entity, and that right certainly does not envision day-to-day decision-making. Rather, the role of the diocesan bishop's supervision as provided for in canon 305 consists in the right of review and approval of statutes, and the right to intervene in case of malfeasance or commission of a delict or abuse of office.

---

24 *VELM* art. 5.

25 See *Final Report Religious Institutions*, vol. 16, 518; https://www.childabuseroyalcommission.gov.au/sites/default/files/final_report_volume_16_religious_institutions_book_1.pdf.

26 Canon 19.

27 See *CCC* 1548; *CCC* 1552. Cf. *LD* 10; *SC* 33; *PO* 2, 6.

28 See cc. 265; 281.

29 See c. 523.

If abuse is committed during work time by lay employees employed by a diocesan bishop, the abuser has the responsibility to repair the damage done to victims. If the abuser cannot or will not repair the damage, the diocese has a moral responsibility to repair the damage done to victims.

5. Obligations of Religious Institutes to Victims

If members of religious institutes (brothers, sisters or clerics) abuse others, their religious institutes have the responsibility to repair the damage done to victims whether it takes place in an entrusted or proper work.[30]

Bishops do not have the power to appoint office holders in a proper work of a religious institute, but merely approve appointees of a religious institute.[31] However, a bishop is usually only informed who the religious institute has appointed. Because the religious institute appoints the office holders, the religious institute holds the liability for any subsequent abuse.

Similarly, if perpetrators are members of societies of apostolic life, their society bears the responsibility to repair the damage done to victims.[32]

If the religious institute does not help the victim or repair the harm done, the diocesan bishop must pressure the religious institute or the Ministerial Public Juridic Person (MPJP) to meet their obligations to repair the damage done to victims. The Apostolic See can force any religious institute to meet their obligations. If a religious institute no longer exists, the diocese must help the victims.

If abuse is committed by lay employees of a religious institute in their proper work, the abuser has the responsibility to repair the damage done to victims. If the abuser cannot or will not repair the damage, the religious institute has responsibility to repair the damage done to victims.

6. Integrated Schools and the Obligations to Victims

Catholic schools in New Zealand have all been integrated into the state education system. This system was changed in 1989 by what is referred to as "Tomorrow's Schools." The government review as part of the Tomorrow's Schools reforms states:

> Until the Tomorrow's Schools reforms of 1989, the governance and administration of New Zealand's compulsory education system was highly centralised. . . . Since the 1989 reforms, each school has been

30 See *CCC* 914.
31 See c. 805.
32 See c. 19.

operating as a largely self-managing statutory Crown entity with responsibility for a wide range of functions that were previously centralised, such as employing staff and developing school policies.[33]

For integrated schools in New Zealand, proprietors, including bishops and religious institutes, have four representatives on school boards. The four representatives are not the majority on the board. The board of trustees in an integrated school appoints the teachers and other staff. If abusers are lay people (teachers, caretakers, etc.) appointed by the board, the board is responsible for placing them in that position. Neither a religious institute nor a diocese makes the appointment and so they are not legally responsible for compensating victims of those appointed by the boards of trustees.

Rev. Brendan Daly

33 New Zealand Government, *Supporting all schools to succeed Reform of the Tomorrow's Schools system*, https://conversation-live-storagesta-assetstorages3bucket-jsvm6zoesodc.s3.ap-southeast-2.amazonaws.com/public/TSR/November-2019/TSR-Government-Response-WEB.pdf.

Canon 694

Ipso Facto Dismissal for Illegitimate Absence

The new provincial administration in a religious institute of pontifical right uncovered the economic crimes committed by former Provincial and Provincial Bursar (while they were in office) and the new leaders followed the canonical process and issued a Decree of Suspension to the former leaders in 2019. Their residence was restricted to a particular community in their Institute.

However, the offenders did not go to that prescribed community for more than six (6) months and were unavailable to the administration for any communication. In the year 2020, when the duration of six (6) months of their unlawful absence was exceeded, the administration issued two (2) canonical warnings (based on canons 696 and 697 - unlawful absence) and sent those letters to the address of that community where they were expected to reside. Because the offenders were absconding, there was no reply to the canonical warnings. Meanwhile, due to the COVID-19 pandemic, the administration was busy with other activities; they forgot about these two offenders and did not take any action on the absent members to issue the Decree of Dismissal.

After two (2) years in May 2022, one of the offenders sent a letter to the Superior General informing that the member would comply with the Suspension Decree and go back to that assigned community to reside. The Superior General forwarded that request letter to the Provincial Superior. The recent modification of Canon 694 says any unlawful absence from the religious institute will attract ipso facto *dismissal.*

Questions:

1. Can the recent modification of Canon 694 still be applied to the offenders even after they sent their request to come back to the Institute?

2. Can the Provincial administration claim that the offenders have already incurred the penalty of ipso facto *dismissal from the institute without issuing the Decree of Dismissal?*

3. Due to an enormous scandal in the Province, the Provincial administration does not want to retain the two offenders in their province. For that purpose, what should the Provincial Administration do?

OPINION[1]

As noted, canon 694 was changed in March of 2019 by the apostolic letter *Communis vita.*[2] Given the new provision in canon 694 §1, 3°, the interplay between canons 665, 694, and 696-697 can get confusing.

Canon 665 §2, which comes under the chapter heading "Obligations and Rights of Institutes and Their Members," tells us that "a member who is absent . . . illegitimately with the intention of withdrawing from . . . the superiors is to be sought out solicitously (*sollicite*) . . . and is to be helped to return to and persevere in his or her vocation."[3] There are no time frames given in this canon, so arguably the obligation for leadership to begin looking for and encouraging the member to return is immediate—as soon as the member's illegitimate absence and intent are known or suspected, perhaps after only a few days. Prudence tells us the superiors should document the measures that they take in their search and solicitation of the wayward member. Once the absence gets more prolonged, attention must turn to canons 696 and 694 since canon 665 is not dealing with procedures for dismissal but rather with the rights if the member and "the institute."

Both canons 694 and 696 come under the chapter heading "Separation of Members from the Institute," and the sub-article titled "Dismissal of Members." Canon 696 (along with c. 697) deals with a penal process and dismissal that is imposed upon a member as a result of his/her actions. In this case the superiors initially thought they needed to initiate a penal dismissal process for illegitimate absence for six months. But they already knew that the members were not able to be located. Should the warnings have been issued at all? Does it matter that they fell on the proverbial "deaf ears?" In the past, before *Communis vita,* this was the likely path for leadership to pursue. With the introduction of canon 694 §1, 3°, a new path has unfolded—one for leadership who cannot issue the required canonical warnings since the member is hiding his/her location. The new text has been translated as follows:

---

1 NOTE: This actual scenario and questions are used here with the express permission of the person who submitted them for consideration.

2 Francis, apostolic letter *Communis vita,* March 19, 2019: *AAS* 111 (2019) 483-484; See also Congregation for Institutes of Consecrated Life and Societies of Apostolic Life, "Circular Letter on Pope Francis' motu proprio *Communis vita*" (8 September 2019), available in *Roman Replies and CLSA Advisory Opinions* 2020 (Washington, DC: CLSA, 2020) 20-27.

3 *CIC* 665 §2, English translation in *Code of Canon Law: Latin-English Edition* (Washington, DC: CLSA, 2020). All subsequent English translations from the 1983 code will be taken from this source.

Canon 694 §1. A religious must be held as dismissed *ipso facto* from an institute who . . .

> 3) has been illegitimately absent from the religious house, pursuant to can. 665 §2, for 12 consecutive months, taking into account that the location of the religious himself or herself is unknown.

The requirement that a member's location be unknown was clarified in a circular letter from CICLSAL in 2019, which stated expressly that: "A person is to be considered unable to be contacted if one knows only a telephone number, an email address, a profile on social networks, [or] a fictitious address."[4] In other words, leaders might be able to talk to the absent member by telephone, Zoom, or Facetime, to message him/her through Facebook or another social media platform, or even to send emails, but still not know the actual location of the member. If that is the case, the member could be considered "untraceable" (*irreperabilitate*), as canon 694 §1, 3° requires.

Generally speaking, once superiors know that a member is intentionally and illegitimately absent, they should document a statement to that effect, along with the date, in order to start the clock running—whether it be the six-month dismissal for cause process (cc. 696-697) or the declaration of *ipso facto* (self-imposed) dismissal following a twelve-month absence (c. 694 §1, 3°). It is imperative that the date on which the absence started be clearly noted.

In our situation, if the whereabouts of the two former leaders had been known to the new superiors—albeit outside the designated living arrangements—and the possibility of delivering written correspondence to them had been possible, then canon 697 would have been the correct canon to consult for how to proceed. Indeed, this seems to be the canon under which the superiors in this situation began acting. They collected proofs (c. 697, 1°) and issued two canonical warnings (c. 697, 2°). However, what is unclear is whether these warnings were canonically correct in how they were carried out: they were delivered to the address where the members were *supposed to be living* but in fact were not living. This begs the question: does it matter that the superiors issued two canonical warnings that were never actually delivered to the absent members? Does it matter that they started off using canons 696 and 697, but then switched over to canon 694 §1, 3°, *ipso facto* dismissal? This switch happened when they realized that the members had been gone for more than twelve consecutive months, and they themselves (the superiors) had failed to follow-up the two canonical warnings with the next step in canon 697, 3°.

---

4 CICLSAL, Circular Letter on *Communis vita*, in *RRAO 2020,* 25.

Clearly, confusion swirls around the fact that both canons 694 and 696 speak of a member's illegitimate absence, and both also reference canon 665 §2. These canons represent two distinct paths to dismissal; the clearest distinction between which process to undertake is whether or not the member is "traceable" (c. 694 §1, 3°). If the member's location is known and delivery of documents can be made, then canons 696 and 697 should be followed. If the member is "unable to be contacted," then canon 694 is in play.

It helps if we look at question number 2 first: *Can the Provincial administration claim that the offenders have already incurred the penalty of* ipso facto *dismissal from the institute without issuing the Decree of Dismissal*?

We will take it as an established fact that all the canonical requirements have been met with regard to the provincial leadership trying to get the members to be reconciled to the community and that the two members intentionally ignored the canonical warnings and other attempts by leadership to persuade the two wayward members to return to their vows. If so, and if the members were absent illegitimately for at least twelve (12) consecutive months after April 10, 2019, then the *ipso facto* dismissal did occur. The canonical process of warnings and the decree of suspension may be part of the process under canons 696-697, but they are not required when it comes to determining whether the *ipso facto* dismissal in canon 694 §1, 3° actually occurred. So, yes, the leaders can—and in fact *must*—hold the members as *ipso facto* dismissed. A decree of dismissal is not required to establish that fact under canon 694 §1, 3°, so yes, the Provincial administration can claim that the offenders have already incurred *ipso facto* dismissal from the institute.[5]

However, this is not the end of the analysis: more is required of leadership after the occurrence of *ipso facto* dismissal. And we can now go back to question 1: *Can the recent modification of canon 694 still be applied to the offenders even after they sent their request to come back to the Institute?*

Upon determining that the members were illegitimately absent, the superiors should have drafted a statement of absence in order to mark the date by which the clock started to run—whether it be on a six-month process or a twelve-month process. A decree of suspension was NOT required under canon 694 §1, 3° for the *ipso facto* dismissal to occur. The fact that one was issued in this case does not seem to have any bearing on the matter. It might be argued that the decree marks the start of the clock running if no such statement of absence was otherwise declared publicly.

---

5 It should not, however, be called a penalty.

The new superiors were required by 665 §2 to solicitously seek out the absent members and to help them to return to and to persevere in their vocations. We have been told that this was done. Additional questions need to be asked, but we will presume the facts support that the provincial leadership was diligent but unsuccessful in locating the absent members, and thus could not help them return to their vows. They even issued two canonical warnings that were never delivered to the absent members. If this was as far as process got under canons 696 and 697, then the return of the members from their two-year-long disappearance very well might mean that the superiors must be allowed to return to the community.

The facts indicate that when COVID-19 hit, the superiors forgot about these two offenders and "did not take any action on the absent members to issue the Decree of Dismissal." We have already established that under canon 694 §2, no decree of dismissal is required. Rather, the *ipso facto* dismissal happens automatically. However, the superiors still need to take action to juridically establish the dismissal. This is another area of confusion; canon 694 §2, says that "in such cases"—seemingly referencing all three subparts of §1—the major superior with the council is required to collect proofs and, *without any delay*, to issue a declaration of fact so that the dismissal may be established juridically. The fact that the superiors were distracted by COVID and did in fact delay—never issuing a declaration of the fact of the *ipso facto* dismissal—would very likely end the case and require the repentant members to be allowed to return. However, the *Guidelines* from CICLSAL titled "The Gift of Fidelity, the Joy of Perseverance" indicate that this is not the case. Rather, when 3° was added to §1 of canon 694 in *Communis vita*, there was a corresponding §3 added to the canon to indicate how the *ipso facto* dismissal was to be juridically established. No mention is made of this being required to happen "without any delay," as is required in §2 for establishing the two circumstances described in canon 694 §1, 1° (notorious defection from the faith) and 2° (attempted marriage). Following is the section from the *Guidelines* that addresses this section of canon 694:

> *The procedure for declaring illegitimate absence from the religious house for over a year*
>
> 86. In the motu proprio *Communis vita* the Holy Father specified, by adding §3 of c. 694, the procedure to be followed in cases where the new case of dismissal for *illegitimate absence from the religious house for more than a year* applies.
>
> The Major Superior has the duty to seek out the religious who is absent illegitimately and cannot be found, and in this way expressing concern for the religious so that he or she may return and persevere in his or her vocation (cf. c. 665 §2).

If the research is unsuccessful, even if repeated over time, or if it is acknowledged that the member is intentionally not able to be contacted, it is necessary "to give legal certainty to the de facto situation."

To this end, the competent Superior:

– is required to produce certain proof through verifiable documentation of the research carried out, and of the attempts at contacting or communicating with the member;

– in the event of a negative outcome of the aforementioned research, the Superior proceeds to declare that the member is unable to be contacted.

The competent Superior evaluates the case with the Council and issue (sic) a declaration of inability to be contacted. This declaration is necessary for making certain the accounting of time:

– the day *a quo*, from which the religious cannot be found cannot remain uncertain, because it would make the twelve continuous month period indefinite (cf. c. 203 §1);

– the expiration of the terms to fix the deadline of the twelve continuous months.

After twelve consecutive months, during which the situation of unavailability of the illegitimate absent member had not changed in any way, the competent Superior must proceed to the *declaration of the fact* so that the dismissal is legally valid, according to c. 694. This declaration must be confirmed by the Holy See if the Institute from which the member is dismissed is of pontifical right, or by the Bishop of the principal seat if the Institute is of diocesan right.

The new provision (c. 694 §1, 3°) does not apply to cases prior to 10 April 2019, in other words it cannot be said to be retroactive, otherwise the Legislator should have expressly declared it (cf. c. 9).[6]

The declaration of inability to be found stating the dates of the illegitimate absence for each absent member and describing the efforts made to contact should be kept in a file along with other related documents in the event that the dismissed member challenges the actions of the superiors. Included in the file should be the documents used to establish the dates on which the illegitimate absence began. Canon 694 §3 tells us that the statement must be submitted to the Holy See (for institutes of pontifical right, as is this case) for confirmation. Thus, in response to

---

6 CICLSAL, *Guidelines* "The Gift of Fidelity, the Joy of Perseverance" (Vatican City: Libreria Editrice Vatican, 2020) 144-146, http://www.congregazionevitaconsacrata.va/content/dam/vitaconsacrata/LibriPPDF/Inglese/dono%20della%20fedelta_ING_testo_stampa.pdf (accessed on 8 Sept. 2022).

the question as to whether canon 694 *can still be applied to the offenders even after they sent their request to come back to the Institute*, I would argue that yes, it can be. Even though the *ipso facto* dismissal has not yet been juridically constituted, there is no timeline given in the canon for this to occur. Leadership can still submit to the Holy See the dates over the course of two year during which the members were absent (with a start date after April 10, 2019) and ask that the Holy See confirm the *ipso facto* dismissal. Note, however, that the leadership will have to inform the Holy See that one or both members has now decided to come back. But the question remains—*back to what*? Have the members returned to their vows, which is what canon 665 §2 requires? It takes more than just returning to a house or the community physically. It requires a return to vowed life and a firm devotion to the evangelical counsels. It will be up to the Holy See to determine whether or not to confirm the *ipso facto* dismissal. So, it is worth pursuing in light of the scandal that has ensued.

Finally, we come to Question 3: *Due to an enormous scandal in the Province, the Provincial administration does not want to retain the two offenders in their province. For that purpose, what should the Provincial Administration do?*

Scandal is never an easy thing to deal with. This question presumes that the Holy See will not confirm the *ipso facto* dismissal. If that happens, the path forward can depend on where in the world this occurred, so I can say only two things:

1) Check the institute's proper law about what it takes to move a member to a different province, and then try to arrange a move. The member may still be under the decree of suspension if s/he is allowed to return, so his/her activities may still be restricted. Not allowing the offenders to live near each other might help deter future wrongful conduct.

2) In the United States, members of religious institutes are subject to civil law as well. There is nothing preventing religious from being prosecuted by civil authorities for egregious financial mismanagement, especially when it comes to harming the operations of not-profit charities. I am aware of a situation where a religious member was threatened with being reported to civil authorities by leadership, so the member decided to seek an indult of departure. Although that might be an option here, one cannot help but wonder if this is the best way to render justice, and whether it is fair to a future employer or to another religious institute who may wind up taking in the member, who could then do similar harm to a business or religious organization.

Lastly, it is important to note that canon 700 also plays a part in cases of dismissal. It was recently changed by Pope Francis such that confirmation of the Holy See is no longer required in order for a decree of dismissal to be effective. The new canon reads:

> Can. 700 A decree of dismissal issued in the case of a professed member takes effect from the time that it is communicated to the member concerned. To be valid, however, the decree must indicate the right which the dismissed possesses to make recourse to the competent authority within ten days from receiving notification. The recourse has suspensive effect.[7]

Before this change, CICLSAL may have been inclined to deny confirmation of decrees of dismissal if the requirement was not met for requiring leaders to act without delay to get the dismissal confirmed. In the present case, two years may seem like a long time for them to have waited. However, we must keep in mind that this was not a case of imposed dismissal, but rather one of *ipso facto* dismissal. The requirement is only that the member be absent illegitimately for twelve consecutive months; the dismissal is automatic. There is no mention of the superiors acting without delay in canon 694 §3.

If the superiors submit their documentation to CICLSAL (as required by canon 694 §3 for confirmation of *ipso facto* dismissals) and it is confirmed, the dismissed members can be served with the notice of confirmation since they now are able to be located. They should be informed that they can take recourse within the prescribed window of time under canon law. Whether the recourse against dismissal would be successful could turn on how solid of a case the leaders have made showing that the members were obstinate in their illegitimate absence for more than two years and how it would be scandalous and harmful for the rest of the institute's members if these two were to be readmitted to membership.

Donna Miller, JD, JCL

---

7 Francis, apostolic letter *Competentias quasdam decerne*, February 11, 2022 (*L'Osservatore Romana,* 11 fev. 2022), English translation at https://www.vatican.va/content/francesco/en/motu_proprio/documents/20220211-motu-proprio-assegnare-alcune-competenze.html.

Canons 764 (*CIC*/17) and 872, 873 (*CIC*/83)

Regarding the Recording of Baptismal Sponsors

In arriving at his new assignment as pastor, Father Tom notices that in the baptismal register, many entries show multiple sponsors for each person baptized. He imagines that this has been a custom for some years in the parish and wonders whether it accords with the Church's law.

Opinion

Regarding sponsors for those to be baptized, canon 873 of the 1983 code states: "There is to be only one male sponsor or one female sponsor or one of each." There is no corresponding canon in the Eastern code.

Canon 764 of the 1917 code declared: "Only one patron, even if of a different sex from the one to be baptized, or a pair consisting of one male and one female, is to be admitted."

Today, in some places, it is common for the parents of the child to be baptized to select more than two sponsors often; as the parents attest, to recognize their own closeness to multiple family members or friends who have played a significant role in their lives. These parents hope that the persons selected to be sponsors will also enjoy a continuing bond with their child.

Those who work with parents who are preparing for the baptism of their children sometimes report that the primary consideration for parents in choosing sponsors is either to "return the favor" to family members or friends who have previously chosen the parents to be sponsors for their children or to demonstrate affection and appreciation for an ongoing relationship. In certain cases, there seems to be an "expectation" at play: they asked us, and now we must ask them.

Canon 872 of the current code indicates that a sponsor "helps the baptized person to lead a Christian life in keeping with baptism and to fulfil faithfully the obligations inherent in it." This is to be recalled when choosing sponsors. It is possible that many of the faithful are not aware of who a sponsor is and what he or she does. And in canon 874, the code spells out the various requirements for sponsors.

From canon 873 we learn that there are to be no more than two sponsors for the person to be baptized. Therefore, no more than two names should be entered into the baptismal register. Homilies and baptismal preparation classes are the ideal place to present the nature of the sponsor for baptism, what requisites are necessary and how sponsors really are meant to assist the parents in their sacred duty of sharing the Catholic faith with their child.

Msgr. Kevin T. Hart, in the *New Commentary on the Code of Canon Law* suggests that when encountering parents who hail from a culture where it is the norm to have more than two sponsors, "it is advisable for the minister to consult with the parents prior to the baptism and determine which two names (one male, one female) will be inscribed in the baptismal register." [1]

Rev. Msgr. Charles M. Mangan, JCL.

---

1 Kevin T. Hart, "Baptism," in John Beal, et al (eds.), *New Commentary on the Code of Canon Law* (Mahwah, NJ: Paulist Press, 2000) 1062.

CANONS 843 §1 AND 915

REGARDING RECEPTION OF HOLY COMMUNION BY INDIVIDUALS IN A SAME-SEX CIVIL MARRIAGE

Among my weekly parishioners are two Catholic men who were civilly "married" to one another many years ago. Should I bar them from Communion?

OPINION

Canon 915 affirms that "those who [are] obstinately persevering in manifest grave sin are not to be admitted to holy communion". This legal prohibition complements the norm of canon 843 §1, which says: "Sacred ministers cannot deny the sacraments to those who seek them at appropriate times, are properly disposed, and are not prohibited by law from receiving them."

At the outset, it must be conceded that any person who falsely holds themselves out to the community *as married* – while publicly living in a manifestly-invalid (in this case, same-sex) "marriage" – could very easily become subject to the prohibition of canon 915. Nevertheless, the philosophical and theological principles underlying the so-called "brother-sister solution"[1] for admittance to holy communion logically suggest the validity of an equivalent "brother-brother" or "sister-sister" solution for same-sex partners in a canonically null "marriage" – and therefore the existence of this potential pathway for resolving irregular unions requires us to proceed with caution, prudence, and pastoral solicitude. For indeed, as the United States National Conference of Catholic Bishops rightly observed in 1973:

> A homosexual can have an abiding relationship with another homosexual without genital sexual expression. Indeed, the deeper need of any human is for friendship rather than genital sexual expression....
>
> On the surface, this may seem like placing the homosexual in a "proximate occasion of sin", but other elements in his plan of life, and spiritual direction, can temper the danger, which is justified,

1 For a more complete review of this possibility under the 1917 code, see Msgr. John Krol, JCD: "Permission to Parties Invalidly Married to Live as Brother and Sister" in *The Jurist* 11 (1951) 7-32. Subsequent papal affirmation was supplied by both Pope John Paul II (*Familiaris consortio*, n. 84) and Pope Benedict XVI (*Sacramentum caritatis*, n. 29).

> considering his need for deep human relationships, and the good which will come from them in the future.[2]

Again, we know that chaste common life (or "simple cohabitation") of an invalidly-married man and woman can be morally justified when for "serious reasons, such as for example the children's upbringing," rather than separating, they "take on themselves the duty to live in complete continence" (Pope John Paul II: *Familiaris consortio*, n. 84). But through an application of the same fundamental principles and logic, it becomes evident that it is also morally possible for a same-sex couple to maintain chaste common life together: when for serious reasons (such as for example the proven experience of loneliness as an even greater danger and temptation toward grave sin) rather than separating, they take on themselves the duty to live in complete continence. We even find a real example of one such arrangement, in the public testimony of one Courage member:

> Matthew told me he had something serious to discuss with me. "I want to become a Catholic," he announced, "I want to go for instruction and be baptized. . . . I also want to receive Holy Communion, and that's the tricky bit. I'm sorry but we'll have to end our sex life. I couldn't possibly go to Communion and be sexually active… [S]o how do you feel about chastity?"
>
> Three days later I went to a full and proper Confession. . . .Over the days and weeks that followed I half expected Matthew to change his mind and recant his wish for chastity. But he didn't. By the end of January he was suggesting we establish separate bedrooms, which we did. Over four months later, our chastity continues. . . . [H]e has found peace for the first time in 31 years and eagerly looks forward to baptism and first Holy Communion.[3]

---

2 NCCB: *Principles to Guide Confessors in Questions of Homosexuality* (1973) p.11. The same document continues (with moral advice equally correct for a heterosexual person):

> If a homosexual person has progressed under the direction of a confessor, but in the effort to develop a stable relationship with a given person has occasionally fallen into a sin of impurity, he should be absolved and instructed to take measures to avoid the elements which lead to sin without breaking off a friendship which has helped him grow as a person. If the relationship, however, has reached a stage where the homosexual person is not able to avoid overt actions, he should be admonished to break off the relationship.

3 Courage International, "Member Testimony: Chris," https://couragerc.org/resource/member-testimony-chris/ (accessed on 22 Aug. 2022). For a similar personal account—instead regarding an irregular heterosexual union—see Father Peter Stravinskas: "My parents lived as 'brother and sister' for 25 years so they could receive Communion" https://www.lifesitenews.com/news/my-parents-lived-as-brother-and-sister-for-25-years-so-they-could-receive-c/ (accessed on 22 Aug. 2022).

An answer to the opening scenario presented above, therefore, must always begin with an acknowledgment that: It's complicated. This is a situation that requires careful dialogue, and a conscious commitment to avoid projecting any uncharitable presumptions. Accordingly, my recommendation would be to begin by focusing on the simpler personal and moral elements:

- How well do you personally know these men? How well do you understand their experiences, desires, and intentions? What is the foundation of their Catholic faith, which they evidently desire to practice? Speak with them – do not guess, or presume to know. Again, while some gay persons are reasonably happy living as single and pursuing celibacy with the support of many friendships, others seek concrete partnership after experiencing the psychological weight of loneliness as a grave subjective occasion of sin.
- Are they already educated regarding the Church's doctrine on sex and marriage? If so, do they disagree with it? Approach them in the same manner that you would approach any invalidly-married couple, and do not assume that they disagree. Some couples will readily acknowledge that their "marriage" is fundamentally a sort of legal fiction, and not strictly a true or ecclesiastically valid marriage bond – and therefore, be willing to affirm that their relationship is properly (theologically) only a sort of *friendship* and *partnership*, whereas their civil "marriage" is fundamentally a sort of utilitarian-financial arrangement, borne out of a desire for long-term committed companionship with legal security.
- If they understand the Church's teaching on sex and marriage, are they striving to refrain from all sexual activity? Are they already living in concrete ways "as brothers" and striving to support one another in pursuit of chastity? If not, are they willing to consider doing so? [4]
- Are they publicly expressing real opposition to Catholic doctrine on the nature of marriage, particularly as expressed in the Catechism? If so, are they willing to cease doing so – that is, to refrain from *public opposition*, even if personal doubts remain unresolved? Might they even be willing to pursue

---

4 If they are unwilling, then it must be said that the application of canon 915 becomes difficult to avoid. Yet we must be very clear that it is at root the *public irregular union* (or, more precisely the *public sexual relationship* implied by the nature of a claim to *marriage*) that impedes reception of the Eucharist. For in the absence of any public sexual relationship, mere suspicion that a same-sex couple is sexually active cannot suffice to justify an invocation of canon 915—just as if one *suspects* that an unmarried person is sexually active, or *suspects* that a married couple is using contraception (due to a "manifest" absence of children combined with an affluent-itinerant lifestyle), it would be absolutely inappropriate to demand a public disclosure or public denial of suspected private sins, or to invoke any application of canon 915 on the basis of a mere suspicion.

educational pathways to help resolve their doubts? Do not presume that the public display of apparent "wedding rings" logically or inherently signifies any public opposition to Catholic doctrine: for—unlike the institution of marriage, which is certainly derived from nature—rings are an artificial and conventional symbol, which could easily be intended (or recontextualized upon conversion) to signify a *public commitment* or non-marital *partnership* that is logically compatible with celibacy.

- If they are civilly "married", are they *in fact* holding themselves out to the community *as married*—that is to say, with terminology[5] that occasions confusion and concern that they have publicly rejected Catholic doctrine on the nature of marriage? If so, are they willing to adopt new terminology (such as *civil union* or *partners*)[6] and refrain from publicly describing themselves as *married* or as *spouses*? Or are there any other public steps that they would be willing to take, to help avoid or remedy any public appearance of rejecting Church teaching? Perhaps at the very least, they could commit to the qualification "civilly married" or "married only in the eyes of the state"—in exactly the same way that a man and woman in an irregular union would (and should) be asked to always qualify their canonically-null civil "marriage".

Practically speaking, if you do not know these men well—if you do not have genuine *certitude* about the *fact* or *obstinacy* of their opposition to Church teaching on sexual ethics or on the nature of marriage—then they should be given the benefit of the doubt (indeed: we should never *presume* sinful behavior or obstinate ill-will on the part of our neighbor) and the broader norm of canon 843 should prevail.

---

5 Be attentive to equivocation of terms, which can hinder authentic communication. This is particularly critical for words like "marriage", regarding which there now exists a grave and radical dissonance between the Catholic definition (in which marriage is *necessarily*, even though not exclusively, ordered toward procreation), and the dominant secular definition (which seems to be exclusively defined as an interpersonal partnership, with absolutely no *necessary* link to procreation). If a homosexual couple refers to their union as a "marriage", consider discussing their definition of that word. Do they concede that there are competing incompatible definitions of "marriage" in our culture today? Do they in fact reject the Church's definition, on a fundamental level—or are they simply using the secular definition for convenience, or out of habit, while not disputing that the equivocation is problematic? "Every good Christian ought to be more ready to give a favorable interpretation to another's statement than to condemn it. But if he cannot do so, let him ask how the other understands it. And if the latter understands it badly, let the former correct him with love." (CCC 2478, citing St. Ignatius of Loyola).

6 For further reflection on the theoretical defensibility of same-sex *civil unions* (as opposed to *marriage*), cf. Ed Peters, "'Same-sex marriage' and 'same-sex unions' are not the same things…," *Catholic World Report*, https://www.catholicworldreport.com/2017/09/13/same-sex-marriage-and-same-sex-unions-are-not-the-same-things (accessed on 22 Aug. 2022).

But indeed, a lack of certitude is not an excuse for inaction; on the contrary, these questions should *motivate* a pastor to reach out, and exhibit genuine accompaniment marked by pastoral sensitivity. Seek to establish a dialogue and pastoral relationship with these persons (if they are open to trusting you), with the goal of arriving at a shared understanding of the moral necessity of abstinence from sexual activity outside of marriage, in keeping with the Church's teaching that all persons regardless of their sexual orientation are equally called to chastity (cf. CCC 2347, 2348, 2359). Listen to and engage with the full complexity of their experience and beliefs, so that any unjust biases or incorrect impressions and presumptions can be corrected, while lines of philosophical and theological agreement or disagreement can be gradually identified. After this, further dialogue and discernment will be necessary for practical questions surrounding access to the sacraments.

For if you find that they are approaching the Church in good faith—if they are not publicly opposed to the authentic doctrine of the Church on marriage and sexuality, and if they are willing to privately strive after obedience to the moral law; or at least if they at least demonstrate a willingness to publicly submit to and refrain from manifest opposition to the doctrine of the Church, while privately embarking on a path to deepen their faith and resolve their private doubts – then in principle they can be admitted to Communion, with due regard for the subjective discernment always required by canon 916. The fundamental principle is that: earnestly striving for adherence to the moral law is always a pathway through which licit access to the sacraments can be restored, at least in private (if not in public, at least where their civil status is unknown, following rules identical to the "brother-sister" solution). For all persons in irregular unions that cannot be regularized—whether heterosexual or homosexual—this necessarily entails: honestly striving for complete sexual continence, while seeking support from the available sacraments of the Church (especially confession, and insofar as possible the Eucharist) to sustain them on this path.

That being said, concerns about scandal (understood properly)[7] to the community might still remain valid, depending on the degree of public knowledge of this irregular union, and other personal circumstances of the individuals involved. But concerns of this sort are not necessarily an insurmountable obstacle: for even if (by hypothesis) danger of scandal occasioned by the public reception of the Eucharist was truly unavoidable, there would always remain the possibility of administering communion strictly in private, where there is no danger of confusion to the broader community. More often, however, it would seem that genuine danger of scandal can be avoided, or otherwise easily remedied, through transparency, education, and clarification: that is, by giving an appropriate explanation to the community (or at least to those individuals who express questions and concerns) while reminding them that we should always prefer to extend the more charitable interpretation to our neighbor and avoid rushing to judgment (cf. CCC 2478).

In any event, *proportionality of public knowledge* is the key for prudently safeguarding against scandal in this manner. That is to say: to the degree that an irregular union is publicly known (to the whole community, or to portions of the community), the danger of leading anyone into sin is naturally mitigated through an equally public disclosure (to the whole community, or to the relevant portions of the community) about what is in fact being done, and why this is a morally permissible arrangement. Those in the community who would insist on "taking" scandal (after being given an appropriate explanation of this sort) are no longer

---

7 That is to say, the term *scandal* must here be understood strictly: in terms of "an attitude or behavior which leads another to do evil" (cf. *CCC* 2284-2287). The broader sense of "an attitude or behavior which causes our neighbor to wonder, or to be concerned, or to be shocked and surprised" – this cannot constitute the sin of scandal (properly speaking) *unless* that attitude or behavior is materially sinful. Otherwise, if an attitude or behavior is materially justifiable or praiseworthy, it can only be said to cause scandal in an equivocal sense. For further theological exploration of the sin of scandal—including the equivocal senses of "Pharisaic scandal" and "scandal of the weak"—see Dominic Prummer, OP (*Handbook of Moral Theology*, nn. 230-232) and Thomas Aquinas (*Summa* II.2, Q.43). For convenient examples of those *equivocal* senses of scandal, see *CCC* 588 ("Jesus scandalized the Pharisees by eating with tax collectors and sinners as familiarly as with themselves"), and CCC 589 ("Jesus gave scandal above all when he identified his merciful conduct toward sinners with God's own attitude toward them"), and *CCC* 1336 ("The first announcement of the Eucharist divided the disciples, just as the announcement of the Passion scandalized them").

properly being "given" scandal, but are responsible for *scandalizing themselves.*[8] And indeed, it should be considered that many couples in irregular unions – regardless of their sexual orientation – could potentially function as a tremendous Christian witness and example to the community: insofar as they might be willing to publicly disclose and witness to their personal commitment to strive to live chastely, in accord with the natural law and Church teaching, as a universally accessible pathway for returning to the sacraments.

These are complex considerations, and pastoral discernment attentive to the complexities of individual circumstances will always be critical. But the fundamental principle remains: whenever we encounter people (especially those on the margins) who express a sincere desire to live according to the Gospel and receive the sacraments of the Church, we must strive to avoid laying down a greater burden than a strict reading of the moral law and ecclesiastical law of the Church actually requires.

Daniel Quinan, JCL

---

8 Compare Aquinas: *Summa* II.2, Q.43: A.6, Objection 1: "It would seem that active scandal can be found in the perfect. For passion is the effect of action. Now some are scandalized passively by the words or deeds of the perfect, according to Matthew 15:12: *Dost thou know that the Pharisees, when they heard this word, were scandalized?*" and Reply to Objection 1: "Passive scandal is always due to some active scandal; yet this active scandal is not always in another, but in the very person who is scandalized, because, to wit, he scandalizes himself." See also *Summa* II.2, Q.43: A.7, Response: "Sometimes scandal proceeds from weakness or ignorance, and such is the "scandal of little ones." In order to avoid this kind of scandal, spiritual goods ought to be either concealed, or sometimes even deferred (if this can be done without incurring immediate danger), until the matter being explained the scandal cease. If, however, the scandal continue after the matter has been explained, it would seem to be due to malice, and then it would no longer be right to forego that spiritual good in order to avoid such like scandal."

CANONS 843 §1 AND 915

REGARDING RECEPTION OF HOLY COMMUNION BY TRANSGENDER AND NON-BINARY INDIVIDUALS

One of my male parishioners has "come out" as a trans-woman and begun presenting socially "as a woman" in accord with their professed gender identity. Another female parishioner was encouraged by this, and now publicly discloses their own identity as "non-binary." Should I bar them from Communion?

OPINION

Canon 915 affirms that "those who [are] obstinately persevering in manifest grave sin are not to be admitted to holy communion." This legal prohibition complements the norm of canon 843 §1, which says: "Sacred ministers cannot deny the sacraments to those who seek them at appropriate times, are properly disposed, and are not prohibited by law from receiving them."

But before beginning to entertain this question—which hinges absolutely upon the premise of some materially *grave sin*—we must first address several individual components of practical morality on questions including: clothing and external appearance, truth and falsehood in language, and medical ethics.

To begin, it must be said that *clothing* and *gendered appearance* are fundamentally matters of social convention: and this, to such a degree that (leaving aside questions of *modesty* and *prudence*) the defiance of social norms surrounding "masculine" or "feminine" appearance (whether breaking them entirely, or simply pushing the limits of accepted boundaries) cannot easily be considered *materially grave sin*. For here there is little (if any) real question of violating a universal norm of natural law morality—as there certainly would be, if we crossed over into addressing questions of sexual activity—but only violations (so to speak) of informal social standards that are (not absolutely, but for the most part) deeply arbitrary and variable.

Indeed it must be observed that, if the case were otherwise—if there were any certain danger of *grave sin* on this point—the Catechism would not be silent on the matter; theatrical cross-dressing would historically have been considered problematic, if not formally condemned; Pope Nicholas I would not have written to reassure the Bulgars that "whether you or your women wear or do not wear pants neither impedes your salvation nor leads to any increase of your virtue,"[1] and the Roman Rota in 1975 would not have opined that "nothing prevents" transgender persons from being permitted to wear the clothing of the opposite sex.[2] The truth is that external elements of this sort (clothing, accessories, cosmetics, hair style, general demeanor) are something profoundly conventional, and they can rarely (if ever) be strictly classified as "masculine" or "feminine" apart from social custom. And it seems the only absolute moral requirement for transgressing social norms in these matters is *having a just cause*; for since (this merits emphasizing, given the acceptability of theatrical cross-dressing) it appears a moral justification for cross-dressing can be obtained even for the sake of something as frivolous as entertainment value, there is every reason to hold that cross-dressing should be (again, setting aside all questions of modesty and

---

1 Compare *The Responses of Pope Nicholas I to the Questions of the Bulgars A.D. 866 (Letter 99)*, Chapter LIX:

> We consider what you asked about pants to be irrelevant; for we do not wish the exterior style of your clothing to be changed, but rather the behavior of the inner man within you, nor do we desire to know what you are wearing except Christ—for however many of you have been baptized in Christ, have put on Christ [Gal. 3:27]—but rather how you are progressing in faith and good works. But since you ask concerning these matters in your simplicity, namely because you were afraid lest it be held against you as a sin, if you diverge in the slightest way from the custom of other Christians, and lest we seem to take anything away from your desire, we declare that in our books, pants are ordered to be made, not in order that women may use them, but that men may. But . . . really do what you please. For whether you or your women wear or do not wear pants neither impedes your salvation nor leads to any increase of your virtue.

Medieval Sourcebook: The Responses of Pope Nicholas I to the Questions of the Bulgars A.D. 866 (Letter 99), translated by W. L. North from the edition of Ernest Perels, in *MGH Epistolae VI*, Berlin, 1925, 568-600, at https://sourcebooks.fordham.edu/basis/866nicholas-bulgar.asp (accessed on 22 Aug. 2022).

2 Compare *CLD* 8:759-760:

> Because, when there is question of *transsexuals*, a radical dissociation is found between psychological sex on the one hand and genetic, gonodal, hormonal and somatic sex on the other hand, so that transsexuals feel like the soul of a woman in the body of a man or vice versa, without hope of being had of a return of the psychological sex to the original sex, nothing prevents predominance from being attributed to *psychological* sex as regards those matters which do not exceed the juridical capacity of the subject. For [instance] "when there is question of ordering one's purely *external* and *social* life, e.g., of wearing men's or women's clothing, of giving testimony in instruments, of the right to determine an heir." However, as regards *marriage*, since there is question of a contract whose essential formal object is the right to acts which are of themselves apt for the generation of children, the capacity to contract it depends on the potency for perfect carnal copula, namely, on biological sex and not on psychological sex.

prudence) something *easily* justifiable when necessary for the sake of mental health,[3] particularly for those struggling with grave and irremediable gender dysphoria or gender discordance. Therefore, this is a matter that cannot rightly be considered to stand as *manifest sin*—much less as materially *grave* sin—for customary standards surrounding the gendered appearance of men and women in no way amount to an absolutely immutable or indispensable requirement of the natural law.[4]

Turning next to questions of language, it must first be noted that any gendered connotation attached to *personal names* is similarly a matter of social convention and custom – there is nothing *properly* "masculine" or "feminine" about any given name. Indeed, it is possible for names to carry no gender connotation at all (Taylor, Jessie, Kelly), just as it is possible for names historically associated with one sex to shift radically and become associated with the opposite sex (Ashley, Morgan, Courtney, Lindsey). There is simply nothing that morally impedes the adoption of a new name – even a name firmly associated with the opposite sex, as experience proves in the case of professed religious taking names like "Brother Mary" and "Sister John Paul". Perhaps the only clear and essential moral requirement in these matters is that there be no malicious deception or denial regarding the technical validity/veracity of other/former names (e.g., baptismal name, birth name and surname, former married name) that a person has historically been associated with. In any case, it cannot rightly be maintained that a public name change as such qualifies as a *manifest sin*, much less a materially *grave* sin.

Regarding the use of gendered pronouns, the matter is more complicated: for here we arrive at questions of truth and falsehood (cf. CCC 2482-2486), and thus – although not every lie is necessarily *grave* (cf. CCC 2484) – we have plausibly identified something at least proximate to material sin, meriting further investigation. Immediately however, there are two significant obstacles on this point. The first obstacle is the fact that human language itself naturally admits of equivocation, and even some degree of evolution: therefore words like "man" and "woman" can (in principle) coherently admit of broader (even equivocal) meanings

---

3 This remains true *even if* we adopt the stricter view suggested by Thomas Aquinas, to the effect that: rather than "a just cause", the moral requirement for transgressing social norms in these matters is raised to "some necessity" (cf. *Summa* II.2, Q.169: A.2, Reply to Objection 3: "nevertheless this may be done sometimes without sin on account of some necessity").

4 I do not wish to suggest that further theological study of this question could not be beneficial—regarding, for instance, whether the Old Testament prohibition on cross-dressing is *strictly* a matter of the old law that has now entirely passed away, or, whether there could still be *some* element of enduring validity rooted in the natural law—but for reasons noted in the text above, and *especially* in the absence of a compelling theological consensus on this point, the necessary legal-moral result is that the benefit of the doubt must be extended (cf. also Rule 9 of *Regulae Iuris*: "Semper in dubiis benigniora praeferenda est sententia").

and definitions, rather than being rigorously tied to one strict definition. Some authors argue that this is precisely what has already happened, and that a formal recognition of this linguistic equivocation is something we ought to be encouraging, in order to help peacefully resolve our modern debates about truth and falsity:

> So these, then, are our two coherent definitions of the term "woman." The first is a biological definition: a woman (1) is someone who has the homeostatic cluster of biological properties that are characteristic of adult human females. With this definition in hand, we can define a trans-woman as a man (1) who wants to be a woman (1) or wants to be thought of and treated the way that women (1) are treated. And now we can give our second definition of "woman:" a woman (2) is anyone who is either a woman (1) or a trans-woman.
>
> . . . .Those who insist that "woman" refers to a biological category are correct. Those who insist that "woman" can be defined in social terms, and that trans-women are women, are also correct. This isn't linguistic prescriptivism: the terms "man" and "woman" clearly are used in multiple coherent ways. We should recognize that this is the case without fighting over *the* definition of gendered terminology. There's nothing to fight over; these words are just being used in two different ways… and context will usually determine what is intended.[5]

If this approach can be sustained, then the use of preferred pronouns is effectively immunized from any claim of *falsehood*: for there is no necessary/logical reason that pronouns *must exclusively* refer or correspond to biological sex, when they could also be understood to refer or correspond (*truthfully*) to an individual's adopted social or legal identity, or even to their internal gender identity, with context determining what the pronoun is most likely intended to signify.

This brings us to the second obstacle, which touches upon a reality that canonists should grasp: and that is the phenomenon of *legal fictions*. For even if it should be conceded that a gender or social identity is strictly-speaking "false", there is nothing that morally prevents us from charitably (even formally) according it some measure of artificial reality. The law is not *lying* when it grants retroactivity of canonical effects to a sanated marriage, allowing it to be legally treated *as if it were* valid from the moment of the celebration of the marriage (cf. c. 1161). Adoptive parents are not *lying* when they claim to be mothers or fathers (unless they

---

5 Matt Lutz, "What is a Woman?" Persuasion, June 22, 2022, at https://www.persuasion.community/p/what-is-a-woman (accessed on 22 Aug. 2022); For a similar argument, see also James Heaney, "Utrum Trans-mulieres Mulieres Sint?" April 2, 2022, at https://decivitate.substack.com/p/utrum-trans-mulieres-mulieres-sint (accessed on 22 Aug. 2022).

actually claim to be the *biological* parents), and we are not *perpetuating a lie* when we omit the names of the natural parents and record *only* the names of the adoptive parents in our sacramental records (cf. USCCB Complimentary Norm: Canon 877, §3).

Again, there is no question of *lying* when we refer to a person by their professional pseudonym; nor when we extend feminine pronouns to inanimate objects like ships or vehicles; nor (during a Latin liturgy) when women are required to say "*non sum dignus*" rather than "*non sum digna*".[6] We are not *lying* (or unjustly cooperating in evil) if we politely extend the title "Father" or "Bishop" to an invalidly ordained Anglican, or when we diplomatically use the title "Mrs." in conjunction with the legal surname of an invalidly-married woman, in order to avoid causing offense. And we have not even begun to grapple with the fact that objections of *falsehood* cannot be coherently sustained against the use of gender-neutral pronouns,[7] which certainly do not *contradict* biological sex. All this being said, reasonable Christians will naturally continue to debate the morality of using "preferred pronouns", and we cannot pretend to definitively settle that debate here.[8] But the point is this: if we *must* analyze gendered pronouns through a strict lens of truth or falsehood, then we must also concede that language and speech admit of various *modes* (e.g. literal, analogical, fictional) – and this fact alone, given the principle that we should prefer to err on the side of charitable interpretation, suffices to prevent us from rashly accusing our neighbor of *manifest sin* without further inquiry.

Turning finally to questions of medical ethics, here it must be conceded that we certainly do find an issue with a clear potential link to material grave sin—for, as the reputed Catholic bioethicist Dr. David Albert Jones helpfully summarizes:

> In relation to the ethics of surgery, the Catholic ethical tradition holds that destruction of a part or function of the body is morally acceptable only when it directly benefits the health of the person as a whole (or at

---

6 For further reading on the history of this question, see Barry M. Craig: *"Non sum dignus/digna:* Pressing out the Female Voice," at https://www.academia.edu/9641523 (accessed on 22 August 2022).

7 Compare the modern resurgence of the singular *they* (mirroring the historical rise of the singular *you*) as a replacement for the "gender-neutral" universal *he*. See Suzanne Davis, "The Astonishing History of Singular They," at https://www.academicwriting success.com/the-astonishing-history-of-singular-they (accessed on 22 August 2022).

8 For further reflection on the competing arguments, see Greg Coles, "*What Pronouns Should Christians Use for Transgender People?*" at https://www.centerforfaith.com/re sources/pastoral-papers/11-what-pronouns-should-christians-use-for-transgender-people (accessed on 22 August 2022).

> least, does not involve permanent harm). This is termed the "principle of totality."
>
> On this principle, forms of gender reassignment surgery that destroy sexual or reproductive function, such as genital "reconstruction", hysterectomy, and double mastectomy, are unjustifiable. Such surgery does immediate harm to the body of the patient while the hoped for social or psychological benefits are indirect and uncertain. Hormonal interventions and cosmetic procedures undertaken in the context of gender reassignment (breast enlargement for example) may not irreversibly destroy function.
>
> [But in summary] … Abstracting from issues of marriage, sexual ethics in a narrow sense, and surgery that destroys sexual or reproductive function, there is no consensus among Catholic moral theologians as to whether an adult who transitions is thereby departing from Catholic moral teaching.[9]

Here, then, is a moral boundary with what appears to be a high degree of certitude: surgical intervention that destroys sexual or reproductive function in violation of the principle of totality is materially *grave sin*. And this is (it merits noting) tied to the same core principle by which deliberate surgical sterilizations of men and women (and other extreme forms of voluntary surgical body modification) are considered gravely immoral, even if not done for deliberately contraceptive purposes. We thus arrive at a complex conclusion: if illicit surgical intervention is *manifest* (e.g. by public disclosure) then it is entirely likely that canon 915 could be rightly invoked by a pastor; but if not manifest, then not.[10]

Navigating the proper application of canon 915 in scenarios such as these, however, is no easy task: for unless there is a just reason to *require* the disclosure

---

9 David Albert Jones: *Gender dysphoria: Some Catholic bioethical reflections*, at https://web.archive.org/web/20210701032528/https://www.bioethics.org.uk/images/user/catholicreflectionsgenderdysphoria.pdf (accessed on 22 Aug. 2022).

10 Again the following examples are a direct parallel: [A] a man who willfully obtains a vasectomy and (for whatever reason) publicly discloses this information—though he would not be required to undergo another surgical procedure to reverse this—must nevertheless (at minimum) genuinely recognize and admit that his choice to pursue surgical sterilization was materially sinful, and affirm his adherence to Church teaching on contraception in an equally-public manner, before he could licitly approach to receive communion; [B] a transgender person who willfully obtains surgery that destroys sexual or reproductive function, and (for whatever reason) publicly discloses this information—though they would not be required to undergo another surgical procedure to reverse this—must nevertheless (at minimum) genuinely recognize and admit that their choice to pursue illicit surgery was materially sinful, and affirm their adherence to Church teaching on this question in an equally-public manner, before they could licitly approach to receive communion.

of private medical information—as there can be, for instance, in matters connected to marriage or ordination—there may be nothing more than mere *suspicion* that a gender-nonconforming individual has pursued illicit surgical intervention, and this suspicion alone *cannot* suffice to justify an invocation of canon 915.[11] Without some factual knowledge based on public information (again, presumably some form of self-disclosure), they must be given the benefit of the doubt—for we should never *presume* sinful behavior on the part of our neighbor—and the broader norm of canon 843 should prevail.

Any practical answer to the opening scenario presented above, then, must always begin with an acknowledgment that: It's complicated. This is a situation that requires careful dialogue, and a conscious commitment to avoid projecting any uncharitable presumptions. Accordingly, my recommendation would be to remain rigorously attentive to identifying what is materially *grave sin* (versus venial sin, or doubtfully sinful, or not materially sinful at all),[12] in combination with what is truly *manifest* (vs. what is private, or suspected), and begin by focusing on the following elements:

- How well do you personally know these persons? How well do you understand their experiences, desires, and intentions? What is the foundation of their Catholic faith, which they evidently desire to practice? Speak with them—do not guess or presume to know. Recognize that while some transgender persons find it more or less tolerable to publicly present (and be perceived) in accord with their biological/natal sex, others pursue some form

---

11 In exactly the same manner: If one *suspects* that an unmarried person is sexually active, or *suspects* that a married couple is using contraception (or that one spouse has obtained a vasectomy or tubal ligation or hysterectomy for contraceptive purposes) due to a "manifest" absence of children combined with an affluent-itinerant lifestyle, it would be absolutely inappropriate to demand this private information, or to invoke any application of canon 915 on the basis of a mere suspicion.

12 Compare David Albert Jones, *Crux* Interview, 26 July 2018:

> Discernment is needed… to distinguish what is sin and needs to be renounced (though perhaps this will only be accomplished by steps) and what is not sin but is an element of diverse and complex human experience. In the case of divergent gender identity, we should not assume, as perhaps the question seems to assume, that someone expressing a deep-seated sense of gender identity is doing something sinful or objectively disordered. On the contrary, the person may be accepting his or her gender identity as something given by God. There are difficult moral issues related to incongruent gender identity, issues concerning marriage, sexual ethics and surgery. Moral discernment is needed to know what can be endorsed, what cannot be endorsed but might, in certain circumstances, be tolerated, and what should be challenged.

Charles Camosy, "Ethicist says Church teaching on gender 'not incompatible' with accepting trans identity," July 26, 2018, at https://cruxnow.com/interviews/2018/07/ethicist-says-church-teaching-on-gender-not-incompatible-with-accepting-trans-identity (accessed on 22 Aug. 2022).

of "transition" (of which there are many kinds and degrees: social, medical, surgical) after experiencing the psychological weight of depression or dysphoria occasioned by intense gender discordance as a grave subjective occasion of theological despair, self-hatred, or self-harm.

- Have they *in fact* already "transitioned," or publicly disclosed plans to do so? Do not presume that self-identification *as transgender* (much less *as non-binary*) logically entails any commitment to medical transition – just as we do not presume that self-identification *as gay or homosexual* logically entails any commitment to engage in same-sex sexual activity.
    - If they *have not* already transitioned (nor announced any sort of commitment to transition) but merely disclosed their identity as a member of the transgender community—that is, as a person who experiences some form of gender discordance—then there is certainly no basis for any immediate application of canon 915.
    - If they *have* already transitioned (or announced some sort of commitment to do so), inquire carefully what this *means*, concretely. What steps have been taken? Are any of those steps *in fact* and *certainly* materially grave sin, not morally justifiable by the principle of double effect? What range of opinions do theological and bioethical experts hold?
    - It is reasonable to have concerns about a member of the community presenting themselves to the community *as a man* (in tension with their female sex) or *as a woman* (in tension with their male sex) – that is to say, with that terminology or behavior that occasions confusion or concern. Nevertheless, it is prudent, and pastorally crucial, to follow the

wisdom of St. Ignatius of Loyola on this point[13] and to remind concerned members of the community that we should always extend the more charitable interpretation to our neighbor and avoid rushing to judgment (cf. *CCC* 2478). That being said, it may be charitable and peaceable to strive for an agreement to use terminology that minimizes confusion or concern in certain contexts—perhaps by more consistently appending the qualification "transgender" or "cisgender" to "man" and "woman," rather than using either of these terms without qualification.

- Is there *in fact* anything "definitively proposed by the Church regarding teaching on faith and morals" that this person manifestly and obstinately rejects, especially in a manner that would give rise to a concern under the headings of canons 750-752? Do not presume that someone "manifestly" rejects any Church doctrine simply on account of their public gender or sexual identity or social presentation. If there is no clearly identifiable doctrine that they manifestly reject, there might well be little if any basis for an application of canon 915.
    - When attempting to identify "the Church's teaching on human sexuality" (particularly regarding questions of sex and gender), rely first and foremost on the Catechism—this being "a sure and authentic reference text for teaching catholic doctrine" (Pope John Paul II: *Fidei depositum*, 11 October 1992). At the same time, acknowledge that the term "gender" is historically novel, and as yet appears nowhere in the current Catechism.

---

13 "Every good Christian ought to be more ready to give a favorable interpretation to another's statement than to condemn it. But if he cannot do so, let him ask how the other understands it. And if the latter understands it badly, let the former correct him with love." (*CCC* 2478, citing St. Ignatius of Loyola). Be attentive to equivocation of terms, which can hinder authentic communication. This is particularly critical for words like "man" and "woman", regarding which there now exists a radical dissonance between the strict biological definition (perhaps more clearly designated "male" and "female"), and the broader colloquial definition (which attempts to understand "man" and "woman" as social roles having little if any *necessary* link to biological sex). Refer again to footnote 5 above, regarding the existence of this linguistic equivocation and one proposed solution for resolving it. Therefore, if a transgender person refers to themselves as a "man," consider discussing their definition of that word. Do they distinguish between "man" (e.g., as a social category) and "male" (e.g., as a biological category), in a manner that prevents them from logically rejecting the material reality of their body on a fundamental level? Are they truly *denying* their biological identity, or do they understand their gender identity as a sort of useful or legal fiction—or even as a truthful expression of an innate psychological experience coequally real and in tension with their biological sex? Do they concede that there is a material-biological difference between a "transgender male" and a "cisgender male," in a way that can serve as a point for common ground for building out further distinctions? Do they acknowledge that it is problematic and incoherent (ontologically, philosophically, and theologically) to speak of a "male soul in a female body" or a "female soul in a male body," even if this description might carry some non-literal, poetic or phenomenological value?

- If you wish to argue that religious submission of the intellect and will is required for some doctrine—"which the Supreme Pontiff or the college of bishops [has declared] concerning faith or morals when they exercise the authentic magisterium, even if they do not intend to proclaim it by definitive act" (c. 752)—be certain that you can identify the authoritative magisterial text and articulate what level of theological weight it holds. Proceed with caution when invoking documents of lesser theological weight that have not been incorporated into the Catechism, *especially* if these sources do not canonically possess a high degree of doctrinal/teaching authority (to be assessed in accord with the competence assigned to each dicastery, in recent history under *Pastor bonus* and its various modifications, and now under the apostolic constitution *Praedicate evangelium*).[14]

Practically speaking, if you do not know these persons well—if you do not have genuine *certitude* about the *fact* or *obstinacy* of their opposition to any verified magisterial teaching on human sexuality, or about any public commitment to certainly-gravely-illicit surgical intervention—then they should be given the benefit

14 For a canonical introduction to these questions, see Kurt Martens: *Nature and Authority of Roman Documents* (CLSA *Proceedings* 69 (2007) 131-164) and Francis Morrissey: *Papal and Curial Pronouncements: Their Canonical Significance in Light of the Code of Canon Law*, 2nd ed. (2001) revised and updated by Michel Theriault (Ottawa: Saint Paul University, Faculty of Canon Law), originally published under the same title in *The Jurist* 50 (1990) 102-125. Here it merits noting that the Congregation for Catholic Education's 2019 document *"Male and Female He Created Them: Toward a Path of Dialogue on the Question of Gender Theory in Education"*—published while that Congregation was functioning under the title and competence formerly assigned to it by Benedict XVI's motu proprio *Ministrorum institutio* (16 January 2013)—was not approved *in forma specifica*, and therefore does not possess any special teaching authority or doctrinal significance that could be held to bind the Christian faithful in accord with canon 752. It is, in terms of theological weight, equivalent to little more than an approved theological opinion—not a document requiring religious submission of the intellect and will, and therefore not a document that can form a legitimate basis for an application of canon 915.

of the doubt (again: we should never *presume* sinful behavior or obstinate ill-will on the part of our neighbor), and the broader norm of canon 843 should prevail. [15]

But indeed, a lack of certitude is not an excuse for inaction; on the contrary, these questions should *motivate* a pastor to reach out, and exhibit genuine accompaniment marked by pastoral sensitivity. Seek to establish a dialogue and pastoral relationship with these persons (if they are open to trusting you); listen to and engage with the full complexity of their experience and beliefs, so that any unjust biases or incorrect impressions and presumptions can be corrected, while lines of philosophical and theological agreement or disagreement can be gradually identified. And perhaps most critically: do not frame your relationship of *accompaniment* as something one-sided or patronizing (as if you were an omniscient teacher guiding a student, with nothing to learn from the student), but rather as a relationship of *mutual accompaniment* in which you each seek to educate and learn from one another in different respects, accompanying one another as equals on a complicated journey.

If you find that they are approaching the Church in good faith—if they are not publicly opposed to any authentic doctrine on human sexuality; if they are willing to affirm the material reality of their biological sex, thus acknowledging and accepting their sexual identity (in accord with *CCC* 2393); if they affirm that they are not denying or otherwise attempting to cancel out sexual difference when they carefully distinguish their sexual identity from their gender identity;[16] if they view their gender identity either as a sort of legal fiction (this being morally justifiable by the principle

---

15 Compare David Albert Jones, "Truth in Transition? Gender identity and Catholic anthropology," *New Blackfriars: A Review*, vol. 99 (July 30, 2018) 756-774:

> There is no high-level Magisterial teaching directly on the concept of gender identity nor is there authoritative teaching on the proper moral theological response to gender dysphoria. This is not altogether surprising as the concept of gender identity was only developed in the second half of the twentieth century . . . and the political and media profile of the issue did not attain its current prominence until the second decade of the twenty-first century. . . . It was not until 2000 that the Congregation for the Doctrine of the Faith offered guidance on canon-legal aspects of "transsexuality" and then only in a sub secretum document for national episcopal conferences, not in a public teaching document. . . . It is only in the past five or six years that there has been any papal teaching in relation to gender identity, and typically this has been oblique.

Ibid. 759.

16 Jones further observes that "there are different forms of gender theory and that some distinction between gender and sex is compatible with Catholic teaching." This, he says, is "implicit in the dictum, 'biological sex and the socio-cultural role of sex (gender) can be distinguished but not separated.'" He continues: "Gender is the socio-cultural role of sex and hence gender is conceptually related to sex and cannot be understood apart from the biological reality of sexual difference. On the other hand, gender is distinct from and is not to be reduced to biology." Jones, "Truth in Transition?" 761.

of double effect, in order to alleviate grave psychological distress) or even as a truthful expression of a real and enduring psychological experience coexisting alongside their biological sex; and if they are resolved to refrain from (or repent of) any certainly-illicit medical interventions – then it would appear they have resolved the essential moral baseline, and thus in principle can be admitted to Communion, with due regard for the subjective discernment always required by canon 916.

In closing, it must be clearly said that: whenever *materially sinful behavior* is manifest, concerns about scandal are *necessarily* real (especially when we are dealing with materially *grave* sin)—for even if no member of the community is actually "taking" scandal, sinful behavior is still actually being "offered" to the community, and thus at least the danger of scandal is necessarily present. But conversely: in the *absence* of behaviors involving true material sin, concerns about scandal in the strict sense are not theologically defensible,[17] and must be answered with an appropriate explanation about the difference between *scandal* and *wonderment*.[18] Those in the community who would insist on "taking" scandal after being given an appropriate explanation (about what is in fact being done, and why

---

17 That is to say, the term *scandal* must here be understood strictly: in terms of "an attitude or behavior which leads another to do evil" (cf. CCC 2284-2287). The broader sense of "an attitude or behavior which causes our neighbor to wonder, or to be concerned, or to be shocked and surprised" – this cannot constitute the sin of scandal (properly speaking) *unless* that attitude or behavior is materially sinful. Otherwise, if an attitude or behavior is materially justifiable or praiseworthy, it can only be said to cause scandal in an equivocal sense. Thus we *can* speak equivocally of "scandal of the weak" – and even affirm a *real* obligation to avoid this sort of scandal out of charity to our neighbor (cf. 1 Corinthians 8:9-13 on eating meat sacrificed to idols) – yet this obligation remains fundamentally conditional:

> Sometimes scandal proceeds from weakness or ignorance, and [in] order to avoid this kind of scandal, spiritual goods ought to be either concealed, or sometimes even deferred (if this can be done without incurring immediate danger), until the matter being explained the scandal cease. If, however, the scandal continue after the matter has been explained, it would seem to be due to malice, and then it would no longer be right to forego that spiritual good in order to avoid such like scandal.

Aquinas: *Summa* II.2, Q.43: A.7, Response). For further theological exploration of the sin of scandal, see Dominic Prummer, O.P. (*Handbook of Moral Theology*, nn. 230-232) and Thomas Aquinas (*Summa* II.2, Q.43).

18 Compare Raymond L. Burke: "The Discipline Regarding the Denial of Holy Communion to Those Obstinately Persevering in Manifest Grave Sin," *Periodica* 96 (2007) 3-58:

> Here, it is necessary to note two meanings of the term, scandal, in Church discipline. The first and properly theological meaning of scandal is to do or omit something which leads others into error or sin. The second meaning is to do or omit something which causes wonderment (*admiratio*) in others... Giving Holy Communion to the obstinately serious and public sinner involves scandal in the first sense.

Available at https://www.ewtn.com/catholicism/library/discipline-regarding-the-denial-of-holy-communion-to-those-obstinately-persevering-in-manifest-grave-sin-1230 (accessed on 22 Aug. 2022).

this is morally permissible) are no longer properly being "given" scandal, but are responsible for *scandalizing themselves.*[19] And indeed, it should be considered that transgender members of the Christian faithful who earnestly strive and struggle to navigate and adhere to the Church's authentic moral teaching could function as a tremendous Christian witness and example to the community, if they feel willing and safely supported in doing so.

In any case, returning one final time to the question at hand: it is the existence of *manifest materially sinful behavior* that must be verified for the proper application of canon 915—and not just *any* sinful behavior, but *gravely* sinful behavior; and this conclusion must be a *truly and certainly* founded in the Church's moral teaching, if it is to safely invoked to justify the public denial of holy communion.

These are complex considerations, and pastoral discernment attentive to the complexities of individual circumstances will always be critical. But the fundamental principle remains: whenever we encounter people (especially those on the margins) who express a sincere desire live according to the Gospel and receive the sacraments of the Church, we must strive to avoid laying down a greater burden than a strict reading of the moral law and ecclesiastical law of the Church actually requires.[20]

Daniel Quinan, JCL

---

19 Compare Aquinas: *Summa* II.2, Q.43: A.6, Reply to Objection 1.

20 A vivid and concrete example of one such unjust burden was recently shared with me by a transgender acquaintance, who earlier this year inquired (via her parents) with a pastor about the possibility of attending Easter Vigil Mass—to be clear: asking simply *to attend Mass*, and even explicitly offering to not to approach to receive Communion, as a compromise in light of having previously been denied communion by the same pastor at Christmas Mass—only to receive the following response from this pastor: she would not be allowed to come to Mass at all, unless she first went to confession and then presented herself according to her birth sex, in accord with a recent diocesan policy requiring all persons to present and conduct themselves in a manner that accords with their biological sex. Now, whether or not the pastor was properly understanding the actual meaning and scope of that diocesan policy (and this is debatable, given the excessively broad wording: "this policy applies, but is not limited to, all Church employees . . . and those entrusted to the care of the Church") is beside the point. For whether this pastor was illicitly acting in excess of particular law, or (though it hardly seems better) "correctly" imposing the requirements of particular law, such a restriction *materially* amounts to a burden *far* greater than that of canon 915, and even greater than the usual effects of excommunication—thus (in either case) unjustly impeding a member of the Christian faithful from fulfilling her canonical obligation under canon 1247. The imposition of such a burden is not only canonically indefensible, but truly scandalous.

Canons 1101 §1; 1127 §3; 1156-1160

Can Couples Renew Their Wedding "Vows?"[1]

Initially, the author indicates that he had answered only in the negative, in a way typical of the positivism of English-speakers, when asked whether couples can renew their wedding vows: couples can not repeat their wedding "vows" in the presence of official witnesses and two others at the time of an anniversary or as a commemoration of the exchange of consent years ago on other special occasions. Under the heading of "Negative" is that analysis. On the other hand, under the heading "Positive" is a canonical argument that would permit the repetition of the "vows."

Negative

Should the "renewal of vows" or "repeating of vows" be desired when celebrating a wedding anniversary, at a retreat, or at another special time commemorating a past wedding by a Catholic, the Church provides alternatives to a repetition of the wedding "vows." The options are necessary because when the actual words of consent are said before a clergyman with faculties in the presence of witnesses, then the canonical form of marriage has been fulfilled. Saying the "vows" equates to always giving new and fresh consent to marriage itself (according to this reasoning). Reading the words in the present tense, a man cannot take a woman to be his wife if she already is, and *vice versa*. There is a presumption running through this negative response that if the couple were to renew consent using the same words for marriage itself as in the *Order of Celebrating Matrimony*, then they could be contracting in the canonical form. This conclusion is drawn from canon 1101 §1: "The internal consent of the mind is presumed to agree with the words or signs employed in celebrating matrimony."[2]

The Church foresees renewal of consent only when there is (at least) a positive and probable doubt about validity or efficacy of the first consent (cf. cc. 1156–1160), and to suggest it in other cases, would seem contrary to the principle

---

1 Multiple canonists have contributed to this answer, not necessarily agreeing, including Rev. Charles Benoit, Rev. Paul Counce, Rev. Benjamin Earl, Ms. Meg Hogan, Rev. Pius Pietrzyk, and Rev. Ken Riley; others have chosen to remain anonymous.

2 See Apostolic Signatura, decree, November 23, 2005, in *Periodica* 96 (2007) 285-288 with an extensive commentary by Navarrete at 289-306 and 307-361; see also Augustine Mendonça. "Defective Convalidation," *Proceedings* 70 (Washington, DC: CLSA, 2008) 193-236.

that marriage enjoys the favor of the law (cf. c. 1060). It appears contrary to the sanctity of the indissoluble bond forged when consent was originally exchanged.

As an aside, in a mixed marriage, canon 1127 §3 explicitly forbids two religious celebrations of the same marriage with the giving or renewal of consent. What makes no sense in that context, makes even less when the two celebrations are separated by decades. Notably, there are existentially two exchanges of consent when a merely civilly married couple convalidates their union.

Since the issue in these references is about the ritual in which a convalidation itself is sought, the argument may be made that "as the 'internal consent of the mind is presumed to conform to the words,' so the words should conform to the intention of the mind." Thus, it may be suggested, the other reasons for the use of the special liturgical rituals at the time of celebration of past marriage should not invoke references to intentional convalidations.

Nevertheless, when the external elements of canonical form are present, even when the "vows are repeated" under canonical form for other purposes, the presumption of validity (c. 1060) would have to be overturned judicially.

There are also some potential difficulties in these special celebrations of the past event with a "present tense" use of the "vows" as in a wedding under canonical form. Those couples who had attempted marriage outside of the Church, even those who are still bound by a previous marriage, would presumptively exchange true consent to marriage in such celebrations using "wedding vows" under canonical form (c. 1101 §1). There are these possibilities:

1. If they are free to marry, then they would validate their consent—they would be canonically married (it would not be registered in the parish marriage register or communicated to their respective baptismal churches for recording there).

2. If they were impeded by prior bond(s) at this "repeating of vows" and the first marriage(s) were then declared invalid, then the presumption of validity would fall to this time of consent since it would have fulfilled the requirements of canonical form. In multiple marriages by those not bound by canonical form (neither party being Catholic), the presumption of validity falls from one marriage to the next as the previous marriages are declared null in succession.

For couples already married in the eyes of the Church and after the special commemoration in which "vows are repeated" under canonical form, if that marriage then failed, a declaration of nullity would be required for each exchange of consent. The presumption would also fall from one repetition of the "vows" under canonical form to the next.

Compared to other sacraments: baptismal promises can be renewed, but the formula "I baptize you . . ." is not repeated. Clergy may renew their commitments, but not repeated are the laying on of hands and ordination prayer. In marriage, a couple may re-exchange rings (such as found in the ritual for anniversaries) and affirm their love for each other, but not repeat consent.

Instead of "repeating the vows" under canonical form, there are special provisions of the ritual book *Order of Celebrating Matrimony* when the intent is to celebrate the past, ongoing marriage (numbers 237-245). Note the words, for example: "special remembrance" (237), "joined your lives in an unbreakable bond . . . now intend to renew . . . promises you made" (240), "by your goodness I took" (242), "who once gave each other these rings" (243), etc., as the past tense of the act of consent continuing from the happy day of their marriage through this desired celebration of the past event and its fruitfulness. One may use the *Book of Blessings* (at #90 ff.), alternatively.

Highlighting for the couple(s) and celebrating community, the actual ritual text for these special rites and the language choices articulated by the Church both demonstrate Catholic belief and more readily accord with sacramental theology (and canonical understanding, too) of the covenant *and* consent of married couples.

Thus, either the *Order of Celebrating Matrimony* (at #237 ff.) or the *Book of Blessings* (at #90 ff.) ought to be followed, with no repetition of consent in the present moment under canonical form.

Positive

Celebrations of marriage anniversaries and other commemorations of the wedding can involve a variety of forms and need not come from currently approved liturgical books. All such services are inspiring and encouraging moments that not only bring pleasure to the couple but serve as a strong witness encouraging perseverance in other couples and the whole Church.

The two suggested texts—the *Order of Celebrating Matrimony* and the *Book of Blessings*—are not liturgical rites as such. Anyone may well construct or compose a prayer service for couples including the marriage vows. Whatever the content, it is a commemoration of the time that has passed since the exchange of consent at the wedding, and it has no canonical significance.

If anyone denounced the exchange of consent at the time of such a commemorative celebration or if it were equated with a convalidation, there is no need of considering an "invalid convalidation" and going against the Signatura and Navarrete. Rather, when the facts bear out that the couple, or one of them, did not know that they were not married, being free to consent to marriage or not, there was no consent. Similarly, if one or both thought that the exchange of consent was a bureaucratically required formality for Church recognition of the marriage by which they were already bound, there was no free consent to marriage. The ground of nullity in such cases is simply *defectus consensus* (lack of consent).

There is no clear and present danger to the repetition of marriage "vows" although some may see the moment as a convalidation.

If a couple could marry and both intended marriage itself at such a commemorative exchange (provided all the requirements of valid exchange of consent in canonical form accompanied it), then a presumptively valid marriage would be the result.

Otherwise, whatever the nature of the prayer service and the words employed, no presumptively valid exchange of consent would result.

Rev. Monsignor Bruce Miller, JCL

CANON 1262

RESTRICTIONS ON FUNDRAISING IMPOSED BY AN EPISCOPAL VICAR ON THE FUNDRAISING ABILITY OF A RELIGIOUS INSTITUTE

The Episcopal Vicar for Religious of a diocese in the United States issues a letter to all major superiors of religious institutes with houses erected in the diocese in which he indicates that, to avoid overburdening the lay faithful, all fundraising activities by religious institutes in the diocese are forbidden. Is such an action a legitimate exercise of governance?

OPINION

In the scenario above, the actions of the Episcopal Vicar are illegitimate and for three reasons. First, they exceed the authority of a diocesan vicar. Second, even if issued by the diocesan bishop, they would exceed the authority given to him in universal law and in the particular law of the dioceses of the United States. Finally, even if such action were legally permissible, it must follow the normal formalities of law to have juridic effect.

As a preliminary note, this question must be addressed with a proper understanding of the nature of the obligation of the faithful to support the Church's endeavors. As the *Code of Canon Law* states "the Church" has an innate right to acquire from the people of God those things necessary to carry out its mission (c. 1260). The faithful are not only free to give to the Church (c. 1261 §1) but are obligated to support the Church financially (c. 222 §1). In fact, this obligation is so strong, it is considered one of the five universal precepts of the Church (see *CCC* 2043). By "Church" the law does not mean merely "diocese". The *Code* states explicitly that, in the context of temporal goods, when it uses the word "Church" its meaning includes every public juridic person in the Church, which includes religious institutes. That is to say, religious institutes have a right to seek support from the people of God in order to fulfill their proper mission. As a part of the pastoral and missionary activity of the Church, the lay faithful have the right, and indeed the obligation, to assist in the work of institutes of religious life and societies of apostolic life.

That does not mean that religious institutes[1] (even those of pontifical right) are free from any episcopal oversight regarding fundraising campaigns. Shortly after the Second Vatican Council, Pope St. Paul VI issued *Ecclesiae Sanctae,*

1 Although this opinion generally refers to "religious institutes" the analysis applies equally to societies of apostolic life.

which promulgated norms for several conciliar decrees. In that Apostolic Letter, he wrote what became the central norm of oversight in fundraising by religious: "Religious may not proceed in the collection of funds by public subscription (*subscriptiones publicae*) without the consent of the Ordinaries of those places where the funds are collected" (*Ecclesiae Sanctae*, 27 §2).

The first effort to regulate fundraising by religious in the United States came with the 1977 "Fund-Raising Guidelines" jointly developed by the National Conference of Catholic Bishops, the Leadership Conference of Women Religious, and the Conference of Major Superiors of Men. Notably, those guidelines required approval from the Ordinary only for fundraising through "public subscription," the same limitation provided in *Ecclesiae Sanctae.* Otherwise, the document clearly understands that oversight of fundraising by religious was to be done through collaboration between religious superiors and the local ordinaries. Nowhere does that document envision the complete prohibition by the local ordinary of fundraising by the bishop. Quite the contrary, it assumes religious are free to raise funds, so long as they properly control and oversee them and communicate to the local bishop the results of their efforts.

In establishing the norm for the 1983 Code of Canon Law, the drafters did not adopt the approach of *Ecclesiae Sanctae*, but rather left it to the Episcopal Conferences to issue particular norms regarding financial appeals.[2] The Congregation for Bishops explained the reasoning behind this canon in its 2004 directory *Apostolorum Successores.*[3] The Congregation there encouraged the Bishops to "carefully consider *in each case* whether there is a real necessity to raise funds" so as not to "overburden the faithful with excessive financial appeals."[4] The intent of the Congregation is clear that there should not be a

---

2 See c. 1262. The restrictions of canon 1265 regarding begging for alms do not apply to this matter. That canon restricts the work of "private persons, whether physical or juridic." Religious institutes are not private persons, but rather a public juridic person. Therefore, their activities as an institute in raising funds are not subject to the restrictions of canon 1265.

3 Congregation for Bishops, Directory for the Pastoral Ministry of Bishops *Apostolorum Successores,* February 22, 2004 (Vatican City, Libreria Editrice Vaticana, 2004). The Directory does not seem to have been published in *AAS*, but may be found online in English at: https://www.vatican.va/roman_curia/congregations/cbishops/documents/rc_con_cbishops_doc_20040222_apostolorum-successores_en.html (accessed on 22 Aug. 2022).

4 *Apostolorum Successores*, 191 (emphasis added). By its context, this direction seems aimed at diocesan-wide appeals, rather than at occasional appeals for smaller parts of the dioceses. Nonetheless, their admonition still holds, that the people of God should not be subject to an unending deluge of requests for financial support.

general rule, but norms that permit such cases to be considered on a case-by-case basis.

The US Bishops issued revised norms in 2002, drawn in part from the 1977 norms, which were given the *recognitio* of the Holy See in 2007.[5] The relevant US complementary norm to canon 1262 concerns fundraising generally but includes two points regarding fundraising by religious specifically. Before addressing those, it is important to note that, by the context and tenor of those norms, the USCCB was in no way intending to prevent religious from fundraising in dioceses. Rather, the norms were understood as a way to ensure that all fundraising appeals would be "truthful and forthright, theologically sound, and . . . strive to motivate the faithful to a greater love of God and neighbor."[6]

Regarding specifically the relationship between religious and the diocesan bishop, the U.S. norms require first, and most relevant here, that any solicitation of funds from religious requires the written approval of their major superior *and the diocesan bishop.*[7] Second, the norms require major superiors to submit periodic reports on fundraising programs to the bishop of the diocese in which those fundraising activities occur. Therefore, under current law in the United States, for religious to solicit funds in a diocese, they must obtain the written approval of the diocesan bishop. Therefore, given the clear language of the complementary norm, an attempt by another of the local ordinaries, whether a vicar general or an episcopal vicar, would be beyond his authority.

Is this then easily resolved by simply having the diocesan bishop issue the prohibition? No, this is more than merely legal formalism. For the law also requires that such determinations must be made on an individual basis, and the reasons for the decisions should be given, at least summarily (c. 51). These requirements are necessary to avoid the arbitrary denial to religious institutes who seek to raise funds.

When the USCCB first issued the new complementary norm, the Holy See requested that the conferences of major superiors in the US opine on them. Both the LCWR and CMSM raised several points of disagreement, but the primary underlying fear was exactly what has occurred in this hypothetical, the arbitrary

---

5 The US Bishops' first norm was issued in 1984 and largely left the matter to each bishop. This has generally been the approach in most other English-speaking ecclesiastical jurisdictions.

6 USCCB Complementary Norm, c. 1262, par. (1).

7 As this complementary norm restricts the free exercise of the rights of religious, it is subject to a strict interpretation (c. 18). This is further reason to interpret the norm as not permitting a diocesan bishop to issue a particular law or general decree prohibiting all fundraising by religious in his diocese.

refusal to permit fundraising. This is the primary reason for the long delay—nearly five years—between the approval by the USCCB and the granting of the *recognito* by the Apostolic See. In order to address the concerns of the conferences of religious, the Holy See recommended a bishop mediator. Most Rev. Thomas J. Paprocki, then auxiliary bishop in Chicago, was the bishop tasked at the time with meeting with religious and mediating their concerns. He wrote about the new norms and the concerns raised by religious in 2008. What he said there is most helpful in this current question:

> An underlying fear behind the reluctance of some religious to seek approval of the diocesan bishop to solicit funds may be an apprehension that a bishop may arbitrarily or even maliciously refuse such permission. If that is the case, all I can say to allay the fears of such persons is to remind them that canon 1737 does provide anyone "who claims to have been aggrieved by a decree can make recourse for any just reason to the hierarchic superior of the one who issued the decree." In the case of a decision by a diocesan bishop, recourse would be made to the Apostolic See, which could be petitioned through the Apostolic Nuncio in Washington, D.C.[8]

As mentioned above, the clear intent of the law requires decisions on fundraising to be made on an individual (*ad actum*) basis, not generally. The diocesan bishop may signal that he intends to reject any such requests made, but he must still decide them individually. When he rejects the request to fundraising, he must have at least a just reason (i.e., it may not be arbitrary). A general letter of prohibition provides no reason as to why the holding of any individual fundraising event or appeal is denied and would therefore be subject to hierarchical recourse, as described by Bishop Paprocki.

Moreover, even if this matter were capable of disposition via a general diocesan norm, such a norm must observe canonical requirements for legal validity. In this case, it would need to be done through particular law or a general decree, not by a letter. Were he to do so, such law or decree must be properly issued, promulgated, and observe the *vacatio legis* of one month. Without these necessary legal formalities, even if this were in the ambit of the diocesan bishop's authority, it would lack all legal force.

In regulating the fundraising actions of religious in his diocese, the diocesan bishop must balance the legitimate right of religious institutes to seek support for their work, the right and obligation of the lay faithful to offer support to the life

---

8 Thomas J. Paprocki, "Recent Developments Concerning Temporal Goods, Including Complementary USCCB Norms" in *CLSA Proceedings* 70 (2008) 271.

of consecrated persons, the bishop's own obligation to oversee the integrity of fundraising appeals, and the danger of overburdening the faithful with an excessive number of appeals for funds. The complementary norms in the United States require that that balancing be done on an individual basis. The diocesan bishop may issue norms on his criteria and expectations, which has been done in several dioceses.[9] However, he may not simply issue a blanket prohibition, which would be an unjust infringement on the legitimate rights of religious institutes as well as the lay faithful.

Rev. Pius Pietrzyk, OP, STL, JD, JCD

---

9 See, e.g., Archdiocese of Chicago, *Policies and Procedures: Book Five - The Temporal Goods of the Church*, §3000 "Fundraising Appeals to the Faithful" (effective July 1, 2000) available online at https://www.archchicago.org/documents/70111/70567/Book+5.pdf (accessed on 22 Aug. 2022).

Canons 1277 and 1295

Acts of Extraordinary Administration by Diocesan Bishop and Transactions through which the Patrimonial Condition of a Juridic Person can be Worsened

Question

In August 2020, Hurricane Laura caused catastrophic damages to buildings and structures of the Diocese of Lake Charles. Hurricane Delta and a severe ice storm brought additional damages to these buildings and structures in October of 2020 and January of 2021, respectively. Besides the consent of the College of Consultors and the Finance Council of the diocese, is any further authoritative intervention required to issue bonds or to enter into a "line of credit" agreement with a bank in order to finance the repair or rebuilding of damaged or destroyed structures, if said issuance of bonds or line of credit exceed the maximum limit established by USCCB Complementary Norm for Canon 1292 §1? The total amount of indebtedness is expected to be $27.5 million, and it is anticipated that an estimated $80-100 million of rebuilding and repair costs will be reimbursed by a disaster assistance grant from the Federal Emergency Management Agency. Thus, it is expected that a significant portion of the line of credit will be reimbursed by these funds.

Opinion

The first line of analysis for the proposal for the diocese to incur indebtedness concerns canon 1277, which states:

> The diocesan bishop must hear the finance council and the college of consultors in order to perform the more important acts of administration in light of the economic situation of the diocese; he needs the consent of this council and that of the college of consultors in order to perform acts of extraordinary administration besides cases specifically mentioned in universal law or in the charter of a foundation. It is for the conference of bishops to define what is meant by acts of extraordinary administration.

The United States Conference of Catholic Bishops approved complementary legislation for the implementation of canon 1277 on November 13, 2007, which was granted *recognitio* by the Congregation for Bishops in a decree dated December 19, 2009. The pertinent passage of the complementary norm for canon 1277 states that, for validity, the diocesan bishop must obtain the consent of the diocesan finance council and the college of consultors when "(1) Initiating a program of financing by the issuance of instruments such as bonds, annuities, mortgages or bank debt in excess of the minimum amount set in accord with canon 1292, §1."[1]

The minimum amount set by the complementary norm for canon 1292 §1 "is $750,000 for Dioceses with Catholic populations of half a million persons or more. For other Dioceses the minimum limit is $250,000."[2]

Thus, the diocesan bishop must obtain the *consent* (not just the advice) of the diocesan finance council and the college of consultors for this transaction as an act of extraordinary administration.

In addition to the requirements for acts of extraordinary administration, consideration must also be given to canon 1295, which states, "The requirements mentioned in cann. 1291-1294, with which the statutes of juridic persons are to be in conformity, must be observed not only in an alienation but also in any transaction through which the patrimonial condition of a juridic person can be worsened."[3]

While the complementary norm for canon 1277 provides a definite monetary amount with a clear calculation for determining what constitutes an act of extraordinary administration, the criteria for defining "a transaction through which the patrimonial condition of a juridic person can be worsened" is a judgment call that does not neatly fall within mathematical parameters.

The *New Commentary on the Code of Canon Law* defines stable patrimony as "all property, real or personal, movable or immovable, tangible or intangible, that, either of its nature or by explicit designation, is destined to remain in the possession of the owner for a long or indefinite period of time to afford financial security for the future."[4]

In an article entitled, "Canon Law – What is Stable Patrimony?" the late Father Francis Morrisey, O.M.I., Ph.D., J.C.D., Professor of Canon Law at Saint Paul University in Ottawa, wrote:

---

1 Canon 1277 complementary norm at https://www.usccb.org/committees/canonical-affairs-church-governance/complementary-norms#tab--canon-1277-acts-of-extraordinary-administration-by-diocesan-bishop (accessed on 22 Aug. 2022).

2 Canon 1292 §1 complementary norm at https://www.usccb.org/committees/canonical-affairs-church-governance/complementary-norms#tab--canon-1292-%C2%A71-minimum-and-maximum-sums-alienation-of-church-property (accessed on 22 Aug. 2022).

3 1983 CIC, c. 1295; English translation by the author.

4 Robert Kennedy, "Title III, Contracts and Especially Alienation [cc. 1290-1298]," in *New Commentary on the Code of Canon Law* (Mahwah, NJ: Paulist Press, 2000) 1495.

> In general, it can be said that stable patrimony consists of lands and buildings, of certain other types of property (such as a specialized library, historical or cultural items), long-term investments and endowments, and restricted funds set aside for a specific purpose. . . . Cash on hand or readily available in banks is not considered to be stable patrimony. It is used for the day-to-day maintenance of the juridic person. Likewise, funds that have simply been earmarked for a future project, but without having been definitively set aside for this purpose are not considered to be "stable." . . . Goods that are not part of the stable patrimony of a juridic person are not subject to the rules of alienation.[5]

In the case at hand, many buildings and structures of the Diocese of Lake Charles suffered catastrophic damage as the result of two hurricanes. Rather than threatening to worsen the stable patrimony of the diocese, the issuing bonds or entering into a "line of credit" agreement with a bank in order to finance the repair or rebuilding of damaged or destroyed structures may be said to be necessary to restore the stable patrimony of buildings and property that were severely devastated by the hurricanes. In fact, it may be argued that *not* issuing bonds or entering into a "line of credit" agreement with a bank would worsen the patrimonial condition of the diocese by leaving many of its structures in a state of disastrous disrepair.

Moreover, it is reasonable to expect that a significant portion of the indebtedness will be reimbursed by a disaster assistance grant from the Federal Emergency Management Agency, however, it is necessary for the funds to be spent before they can be reimbursed. As such, the proposed indebtedness in this case should not be considered "a transaction through which the patrimonial condition of a juridic person can be worsened" and thus the requirements for alienation mentioned in canons 1291-1294 need not be observed.

The proposed indebtedness should be understood only as an act of extraordinary administration for which the diocesan bishop must obtain the *consent* of the diocesan finance council and the college of consultors.

Most Rev. Thomas John Paprocki, STL, MBA, JD, JCD

---

5 Francis Morrisey, "Canon Law—What Is Stable Patrimony?" in *Health Progress* (March-April 2008) at https://www.chausa.org/publications/health-progress/article/march-april-2008/canon-law---what-is-stable-patrimony- (accessed on 22 Aug. 2022).

TRADITIONIS CUSTODES

CONCERNING THE SACRAMENTAL VALIDITY OF THE 1962 LITURGICAL TEXTS

Does the introduction of new sacramental forms by Paul VI in Divinae Consortium Naturae *and* Sacram Unctione Infirmorum *thereby invalidate those found in the unrevised* Rituale Romanum*?*

OPINION

This brief response is only to discuss the question of sacramental validity and not a question of liceity subsequent to the 2021 *motu proprio* of Pope Francis, *Traditionis Custodes*.

Subsequent to the Second Vatican Council, the forms of a number of sacraments underwent changes within the Roman Rite:

1) The Holy Eucharist, in two ways:

- By an expanded "institution narrative" which enlarged what are understood as the *verba consecrationis*;
- The words "*mysterium fidei*" were removed from the words of consecration of the chalice.

2) Confirmation

- 1962: N. *Signo te signo Cru + cis, et confírmo te Chrísmate salútis: In nómine Pa + tris, et Fí + lii, et Spíritus + Sancti. Amen.*
- 1971: *Accipe signaculum Doni Sancti Spiritus Sancti.*

3) Extreme Unction

- 1962: *Per istam sanctam Unctió + nem, [et suam piíssimam misericórdiam – omitted in the emergency formula], indúlgeat tibi Dóminus quidquid per [visum, auditum, odoratum, gustum et locutionem, tactum, gressum] deliquísti. Amen.*
- 1972: *Per istam sanctam Unctionem et suam piissimam misericordiam adiuvet te Dominus gratia Spiritus Sancti, Ut a peccatis liberatum te salvet atque propitius alleviet. Amen.*

4) Holy Orders (ordination/consecration of a bishop)

- 1962: *Vere dignum et justum est, æquum et salutáre, nos tibi semper, et ubíque grátias ágere, Dómine sancte, Pater omnípotens, ætérne Deus, honor ómnium dignitátum, quæ glóriæ tuæ sacris famulántur ordínibus.*

Deus, qui Móysen fámulum tuum secréti familiáris affátu, inter cætera cœléstis documénta cultúræ, de hábitu quoque induménti Sacerdotális instítuens, eléctum Aaron mystico amíctu vestíri inter sacra jussísti, ut intelligéntiæ sensum de exémplis priórum cáperet secutúra postéritas, ne erudítio doctrínæ tuæ ulli deésset ætáti ... Multíplica super eum bene + dictiónem et grátiam tuam: ut ad exorándam semper misericórdiam tuam tuo múnere idóneus et tua grátia possit esse devótus. Per Dominum ....

- 1968: *Et nunc effunde super hunc electum eam virtutem, quae a te est, Spiritum principalem, quem dedisti dilecto Filio Tuo Jesu Christo, quem ipse donavit sanctis Apostolis, qui constituerunt Ecclesiam per singula loca, ut sanctuarium tuum, in gloriam et laudem indeficientem nominis tui.*

From a basic juridical perspective, in the promulgation of these new sacramental forms subsequent to the Council by Paul VI (in particular, concerning Confirmation in *Divinae Consortium Naturae* and Anointing of the Sick in *Sacram Unctione Infirmorum*) there was no invalidating clause attached whatsoever (cf. canon 14 CIC/83; canon 11 CIC/17).

Within the theological tradition, St. Thomas Aquinas speaks of alterations to the form of the sacraments, such as baptism, which would invalidate the form in *Summa Theologiae*, IIIa, q. 60, a. 7, particularly in his responses to the objections. Citing St. Augustine, he argues in the reply to Objection 1 that "the word operates in the sacraments 'not because it is spoken ... but because it is believed' in accordance with the sense of the words which is held by faith." Since the sacraments (and their forms) express the perennial faith of the Church, the forms must express this faith, although they may do so in varying ways.

The Latin Church, in her liturgical praxis, has enjoyed the usage of various sacramental forms. Felix Cappello SJ teaches that aside from what has been defined by the Council of Trent, the Church could very probably at one point in time indicate different sacramental forms for, for instance, the Latin Church and the Eastern Churches.[1] Indeed, the Eastern churches generally use passive grammatical forms for their sacramental formulae. Even within the Latin Church, absolution in the Dominican Rite not only alters the ordering of the most essential words of absolution (from "*ego te absolvo*" to "*ego absolvo te*"), but also includes different words and three signs of the Cross, whereas the Roman Rite contains only one. In both cases, the sacramental signification has been considered by the

1 F. Cappello, *Tractatus Canonico-Moralis de Sacramentis*. vol. 1: *De Sacramentis in Genere* (Turin-Rome: Marietti, 1953) 22.

Church to be identical. More specifically, in relation to the revised post-conciliar rites, Pope Paul VI noted on 19 November 1969, at the time of the promulgation of the *Novus Ordo Missae*, that "the unity of the Lord's Supper, of the Sacrifice on the Cross, and of the re-presentation and the renewal of both in the Mass, is inviolably affirmed and celebrated in the new rite just as they were in the old." They maintain the same sacramental signification, maintaining the same Catholic faith, despite verbal variations.

Cappello likewise provides six (6) categories of possible mutations in the sacramental form: additions, subtractions, corruptions of words, transpositions of words, changes of words, and interruptions, and provides the circumstances in which these may or may not impact the sacramental form.[2] Invalidating alterations, in general, stem from the intention of the minister to introduce a heretical interpretation, which would change the signification of the sacramental sign itself. For instance, changing the form of baptism from "I baptize you" to "We baptize you" would imply an erroneous notion that the community is the one conferring the sacrament rather than the specific minister of the sacrament.

It should be noted that even subsequent to *Traditionis Custodes*, the 1962 *Missale Romanum*, with its differing form of consecration of the Eucharist, is still being used (as all of these sacramental rites have been used) side-by-side within the Roman Rite, on a general basis since *Summorum Pontificum* and *Universae Ecclesiae*. *Traditionis Custodes*, being a restrictive document which must be read restrictively, does not itself in any way place restrictions upon the use of any of the other liturgical books of 1962, including the *Rituale* or *Pontificale*. Thus, a lower authority in the Church, particularly one without legislative authority (in this case, the Congregation for Divine Worship and the Discipline of the Sacraments) would not have the authority to place restrictions thereupon. These liturgical texts are also still being used by the Society of St. Pius X, to whom Pope Francis has granted all necessary faculties for sacramental ministry during the 2015 Year of Mercy. The validity of their usage of these sacramental forms has never been called into question, despite their canonically irregular status.

Arguing from the above-cited text of Paul VI, on the basis of the diachronic continuity and identity of the Church's *lex orandi* and *lex credendi*, consequently, it cannot be held that a juridical restriction, regardless of stringency, placed upon the use of a liturgical text in any way impacts the sacramental validity of the altered sacramental form. Perhaps the best way to understand, then, the novel sacramental forms issued by Paul VI is that they were conceived in order to correspond to the reformed rites – as, indeed, Paul VI himself notes in the

2 Cappello, 17-18.

Apostolic Constitutions issuing these changes. In point of fact, even during the years in which the unrevised books were not in general usage (i.e. 1971 until 1988), to this author's knowledge, sacraments (perhaps illicitly) conferred according to the former liturgical forms were never judged on that basis to be invalid. Thus, the revised forms were never imposed upon the Western Church under pain of sacramental invalidity.

With all of these things established, this author humbly parts company with the opinion of Cappello to argue, from perhaps a more theological-juridical perspective, that the Church cannot legislatively declare a sacramental form in immemorial usage to be invalid, nor restrict entirely all use thereof. Indeed, as Cardinal Ratzinger affirmed, "Rites ... are forms of the Apostolic Tradition and of its unfolding in the great places of the Tradition."[3] These rites are places, or monuments, where the Apostolic Tradition may be found.

In conclusion, it is the opinion of this canonist that the liturgical books of the Roman Rite (be they the editions of what are commonly called the extraordinary or ordinary forms), in their editions which have been duly approved by the proper hierarchical authorities, whether in Latin or in the vernacular, can be used without scruple of conscience or doubt concerning sacramental validity.

Rev. Albert P. Marcello, III, JCD (Cand.)

---

3 Joseph Ratzinger, *The Spirit of the Liturgy* (San Francisco: Ignatius Press, 1999) 163-164.

CONTRIBUTORS

Very Rev. Patrick Cooney, OSB, JCL, is the Judicial Vicar for the Diocese of Owensboro, Kentucky.

Rev. Msgr. Brendan P. Daly, JCD, is Judicial Vicar for the Tribunal of the Catholic Church in New Zealand and a lecturer in canon law at Good Shepherd College.

Rev. Msgr. Charles M. Mangan, JCL, is from the Diocese of Sioux Falls and is on the faculty of Mt. St. Mary's Seminary in Emmitsburg, MD.

Rev. Albert P. Marcello, III, JCD (Cand.) is from the Diocese of Providence and a JCD candidate at the Katholieke Universiteit, Leuven.

Rev. Msgr. Bruce Miller, JCL, is from the Diocese of Alexandria, LA, and is a past President of the Canon Law Society of America.

Hon. Donna Miller, JD, JCL, is the Executive Coordinator for the Canon Law Society of America residing in The Villages, FL.

Most Rev. Thomas John Paprocki, STL, MBA, JD, JCD, is the Bishop of Springfield in Illinois and Adjunct Professor of Law at Notre Dame Law School.

Rev. Pius Pietrzyk, OP, STL, JD, JCD, is Adjunct Professor of Canon Law at the Pontifical Faculty of the Immaculate Conception in Washington, DC.

Daniel Quinan, JCL, is a judge for the Archdiocese of Minneapolis and St. Paul.

Rev. Msgr. Michael A. Souckar, JCD, is the Adjutant Judicial Vicar for the Archdiocese of Miami, Florida, and Pastor of St. Andrew Catholic Church in Coral Springs, Florida.

Made in United States
North Haven, CT
10 November 2026

22088262R00065